TRADITIONAL QUILTS

TODAY'S TECHNIQUES

DEBRA WAGNER

**krause
publications**

since
1952

700 E. State Street • Iola, WI 54990-0001

krause publications

700 E. State Street • Iola, WI 54990-0001
Telephone: 715/445-2214

Please call or write for our free catalog of publications.
Our toll-free number to place an order or obtain a free catalog is 800-258-0929
or please use our regular business telephone 715-445-2214 for editorial comment and further information.

Designed by Stan Green/Green Graphics
Cover Design by Anthony Jacobson
Manufactured in the United States of America

Library of Congress Cataloging-in-Publication Data

Wagner, Debra.
    Traditional quilts : today's techniques / Debra Wagner.
        p.   cm.
    Includes bibliographical references and index.
    ISBN 0-8019-8660-5
    1. Machine quilting. 2. Machine appliqué. I. Title.
TT835.W3323   1997
746.46—dc21   96-29945
                                                                  CIP

1 2 3 4 5 6 7 8 9 0   6 5 4 3 2 1 0 9 8 7

Acknowledgments

I would like to thank the sewing machine companies and dealerships, and the staff who helped me research the feet and stitches in this book:

 Baby Lock
 Bernina of America
 Brother International Corporation
 Elna Sewing Machine Company
 New Home Sewing Machine Company
 Pfaff American Sales Corporation
 Riccar
 Viking Husqvarna

In addition, I would like to thank:

Debbie Casteel, for her generous help in suggesting solutions and products to improve my appliqué;

Jan Dalton at Curiosity, for sharing her appliqué placement method with me, and allowing me to pass that information along to you;

Elizabeth Bradley, a British needlepoint designer whose designs and color choices are a constant inspiration to me;

Elly Sienkiewicz, author and historian who specializes in Baltimore Album quilts of the 19th century: her books and hand sewing methods inspired many of my techniques in this book;

Rosalie Cooke, for her help in editing this book.

Contents

PART ONE: MACHINE SMARTS

PART TWO: FABRIC PREPARATION FOR APPLIQUÉ

Chapter 5

Raw-Edge Appliqué 41

PART THREE:
APPLIQUÉ STITCHES & STITCHING

Chapter 6

Invisible Stitches for Appliqué 51

Chapter 7

Decorative Stitches for Appliqué 63

Chapter 8

The Buttonhole Stitch 75

Chapter 9

Duplicating Hand Stitches 85

Chapter 10

Decorative Satin Stitching 91

PART FOUR: QUILT BINDINGS

Chapter 15

Odds and Ends 148

PART FIVE:
APPLIQUÉ PATTERNS

Chapter 16

Appliquéd Baskets and Christmas Wreath 159

Introduction

Chances are, you use a sewing machine to make quilts and know how machine quiltmaking has moved to the forefront. Piecing, quilting, and appliqué can all be done on today's sewing machines. Within the last decade our machines have become sophisticated and user-friendly, and the possibilities the machine offers are pushing quiltmaking in new directions. Yet the volume of new information and techniques makes it impossible for average owners to realize the full potential of their machines.

As quilt makers, we tend to overlook the myriad of feet, accessories, and stitches that the machine manufacturers have designed to simplify our work. We limit ourselves to basic $1/4$" seams or free-motion quilting. But, those techniques are barely the beginning.

For example, did you know there are ways to machine stitch both edges of the rod pockets to the quilt back? That you can make perfect $1/16$" stems for hand or machine appliqué using your buttonhole or pintuck foot? Do you know how to use mini rickrack to make a binding that looks like tiny prairie points? Even a basic machine is capable of making these and many more intricate and breathtaking effects. Best of all, these techniques don't require a Ph.D. in machine mechanics or months of practice.

In this book I have collected the best of machine techniques. They come from my 30 years in the sewing field. Inspiration comes from sewing machine manufacturers and the dazzling array of new machine features. Some techniques are based on recent innovations in the sewing field. A few techniques come from the owner's guides of treadle machines. If you use a sewing machine to make quilts, this book is for you. No matter the age of your machine or its number of stitches, you will find techniques that can help your quiltmaking.

LET ME ENCOURAGE YOU TO MAKE SAMPLES

For years I have made and kept samples of new techniques. I learned to sew by making samples.

As a sewing machine dealer, my mother was constantly trying out new techniques to improve her sewing classes. It was impossible to make projects for every technique, the only alternative was to make samples. She has notebooks full of every conceivable sewing technique. The notebooks serve as an easy way to combine techniques from dozens of sources into an easy-to-use reference.

When I started to sew, it seemed normal for me to make samples before starting a new project. These samples serve as an invaluable reference to my sewing skills. I think that samples are the most important learning tool a stitcher can use. Samples have many advantages over making projects:

❑ Samples are small, simple, less than perfect trials of a sewing technique.

❑ The small size of the samples allows you to try out techniques without investing much money or time.

❑ You can move quickly through the basic steps of the technique before making a major commitment.

As you make the sample, you can adapt techniques and methods to your machine and your sewing skill level. Many times I have tried a new technique only to realize that I would like to change the directions to fit my skills. Maybe there is a single step that just doesn't work. In a sample, you find that out before you are in the middle of the project.

Samples give you the freedom to make mistakes. If something doesn't work the first time, you can throw the sample away and move on to another sample, until you get it right—or you might want to keep your mistakes. Sometimes

I learn more from my "goofs" than from all my "perfect" stitching. Mistakes highlight places that can be troublesome. Samples can be used to find the creative ways to correct future errors, and sometimes lead to completely new techniques. Think of the sample as a playground. Use it to build skills and to have fun.

Best of all, samples provide you with a tactile example of the technique. Words can't convey all the information you get in a single sample. Most of us learn best by doing, seeing, and touching. Looking at a sample quickly brings the information to mind without you having to thumb through a dozen pages of text. By keeping the samples with their handwritten notes, you have an excellent record of each new technique. You might also want to add pages of directions or ideas from books and magazines.

Think of this as a samples book; you're learning techniques that you can apply to any project you like, whether it's a quilt or wearable art. I have given instructions for making samples for every technique. The samples give you an easy, quick way to learn new methods. The samples in one chapter may carry over to the following chapters. In the appliqué sections, the samples show you how to prepare the appliqué pieces for stitching. In the next chapters you use the prepared appliqué pieces to practice stitching the appliqué in place. (Photographs of my own samples, complete with imperfections, are scattered throughout this book.)

I suggest you start your own sample collection. It is important that the samples be stored in a logical, easy-to-access system. I use two methods to store my sample collection. For small samples, I use a three ring note-

book and place the fabric samples in plastic pockets. For larger samples, I place the fabrics in a sturdy covered box. This helps to keep like things together, and makes the information easy to access.

HOW TO USE THIS BOOK

This is a techniques book, similar to an advanced owner's guide for your sewing machine. I feature machine feet, accessories, and stitches, and give clear, complete directions on how to use them in quiltmaking techniques. I make these techniques workable for the average quilter. The information is in a generic format that covers most types of machines, though occasionally there is brand-specific information. The techniques are applicable to machine appliqué, embroidery, and binding, and there are even ideas that will appeal to traditional hand quilters.

In general, I assume you own a sewing machine and have used it at least once in the last few months. You should know how to turn the machine on, change feet, adjust the stitch width and stitch length, and choose basic stitches. You should also know basic quilt making skills:

❑ How to prewash and preshrink your fabrics.

❑ How to use a rotary cutter, rulers, and mat.

❑ How to stitch accurate seam allowances.

HOW THE BOOK IS ORGANIZED

PART ONE focuses on the stitches, features, and presser feet that you will find indispensable in your quiltmaking.

PART TWO offers a variety of

machine appliqué techniques for both turned-edge and raw-edge appliqué. I assume you are familiar with the basics of appliqué, including layering, overlaps, and transferring the pattern to the background fabric.

PART THREE has detailed instructions for stitching appliqués to the background fabrics with the buttonhole stitch, and illustrates ways to embellish appliqué using decorative stitches.

PART FOUR describes machine-made bindings. There is something for everyone, from the rank beginner to the professional.

It finishes with a chapter on the details of machine finishing your quilts.

PART FIVE has a selection of appliqué patterns.

MARGIN ICONS

To help you use the information, I've marked some topics as follows:

Caution

Marks places that can be the cause of problems. I tell you what to look for and how to stay away from disaster.

Hot Tip

Special tips that expand on common quilting techniques, ideas, or materials. They offer new or better ways to do the ordinary.

Machine Savvy

Technical information about using your sewing machine, including expanded explanations for settings, techniques, or supplies. You can skip these explanations if you feel comfortable with the general information. You might find the extra explanation interesting if you are the type who wants to know *everything* and likes to impress your friends.

Sew A Sample

Indicates a great place to make a sample of the techniques. Samples give you practice and allow you to finetune the directions before moving on to a "real" quilt. Write the machine settings directly on the fabric. Also write reference

notes, like the year, the source of the technique, the threads, and even fabric preparation. The key is to write down anything you need to recreate your success. That way you have a visual record of all your new skills, and your own notes and suggestions to make them work best on your machine.

Sewing Savvy

Sewing hints, explanations, and techniques that many quilters already know. You might find something new and interesting even if you are an experienced quilter.

My best description of this book's intent is "better and more." Your stitching will be better and more accurate. In addition, you will be able to make more, have more time, and be more creative. This book is a collection of my best techniques. It has been a pleasure to write. I hope it will be as enjoyable for you to use.

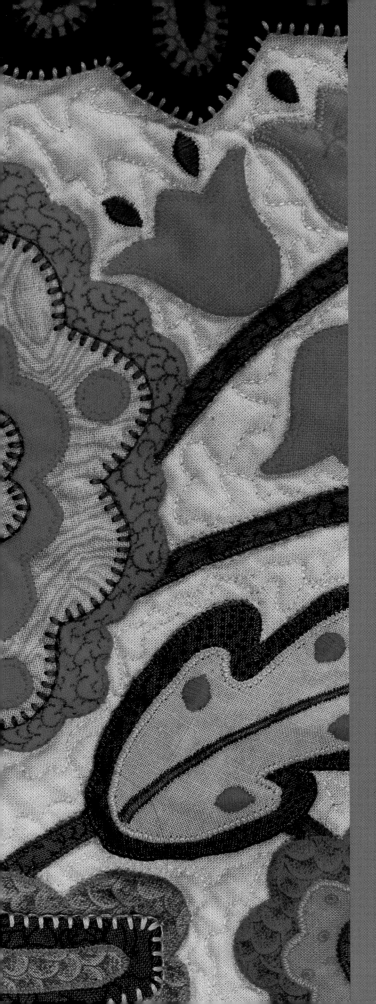

Part One

Machine Smarts

CHAPTER 1
Sewing Machine Stitches and Features

CHAPTER 1 FOCUSES ON the stitches and sewing machine features used throughout the book. Before reading this chapter, find your machine's instruction book, all the accessories, and any additional information like the advanced owner's manuals.

The following sections describe possible stitches, explain mechanical features, and discuss accessories for sewing machines. This is a generic list for any age or model of machine. Don't think of it as a requirement list, but simply a "hunting expedition" checklist to learn what your machine does, and how it works. Remember that this list does not in any way reflect the quality of the machine. No single machine has every feature or accessory. Every machine does things slightly differently, and every machine has its own vocabulary of names for its features and stitches. Most important, don't worry if your machine doesn't have a feature or foot. Alternative stitches or feet give the same results for each technique.

STRAIGHT STITCH

The most used stitch is the straight stitch. There are two variables for

the straight stitch: the stitch length and the needle position.

It is important to know the maximum, minimum, and average stitch length on your machine. The stitch length is measured in millimeters (mm), stitches per inch (spi), or uses independent scales. Compare the measurements of two scales:

Millimeters (mm)	Stitches per inch (approximate)
.5	50
1	25
1.5	16
2	12
2.5 (asl)	10 (asl)
3	8
3.5	7
4	6
4.5 to 5	5
5.5 to 6	4

asl=average stitch length

It is also important to know if your machine has more than one needle position for straight

stitching. Common needle positions include left (L), center (C) and right (R).

STITCH LENGTH

Stitches per inch scale. Stitches per inch (spi) is a common scale for older model machines. Small stitches give you 22 stitches per inch, while long stitches can give you 4 to 6 stitches per inch.

Metric scale (millimeters). The metric scale is common on new machines and is the scale I use throughout the book. It is a logical system based on millimeters. (I know most Americans panic at the thought of metrics. Just remember $1/4$" equals about 6 millimeters.) The number on the dial indicates the length of each stitch when sewn on two layers of medium weight cotton fabric. For example:

1.0 = 1 millimeter length

2.0 = 2 millimeters length

3.0 = 3 millimeters length
or ⅛" inch long

4.0 = 4 millimeters length

Independent scales. Some machines do not use a standardized scale of stitch lengths. Some use a numbered system; some, a series of pictures. This can make it difficult to translate generic directions to your machine. To correlate your machine's scale to a metric or spi scale may require a little work. First, I recommend checking in the owner's manual. If you are lucky, the manual explains how the scale relates to stitches per inch or metrics. If you can't find that information make a stitch length sample.

Sew A Sample

Supplies

• 6" x 3" piece of light-colored cotton broadcloth

• 1 piece of typing paper

Machine Setup

Thread the machine with contrasting thread in the bobbin and in the needle. Mismatched thread makes it easier to see the individual stitches.

On the right side of the fabric, using a pencil, draw 5 lines 1" apart, or use 1" check gingham (see Fig. 1-1). Place the typing paper under the fabric when stitching. Sew through the paper and the fabric. The paper makes it easier to see and count the stitches.

Set the machine for a different stitch length in each inch section, then count the number of stitches between the lines to determine the

stitch length in stitches per inch. (I recommend starting to stitch on the longest stitch length and working to shorter stitch lengths.)

1 Set the machine for the longest straight stitch.

2 Stitch from the first line to the second line. Let the machine feed the fabric. Don't pull or push on the fabric; just gently guide it.

3 Write the stitch length on the fabric next to the line of stitching.

4 At the second line, stop sewing and shorten the stitch length to a smaller setting.

5 Sew one inch at this setting.

6 Write this length on the

fabric next to this portion of the stitching.

7 Continue adjusting the stitch length and recording the stitch length number. When you reach the end of the first line, continue stitching in a second row of sample lengths, next to the first row.

8 Remove the sample from the machine and use a magnifying glass to count the number of stitches in each marked inch. I know it can be difficult to accurately count the shorter stitch lengths. I suggest you make a guess on the shorter stitches per inch, based on the longer lengths. The average stitch length is 10 stitches to the inch.

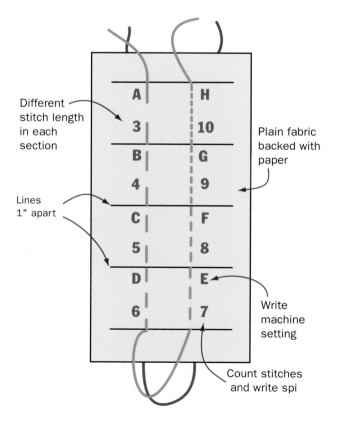

Different stitch length in each section

Lines 1" apart

Plain fabric backed with paper

Write machine setting

Count stitches and write spi

A	H
3	10
B	G
4	9
C	F
5	8
D	E
6	7

Fig. 1-1

NEEDLE POSITIONS

Needle position refers to the location of the needle in relationship to the center of the presser foot and needle hole opening. Use needle positions with both straight stitch and zigzag stitch. In straight stitch, the needle positions produce accurate topstitching and adjustable seam allowances. In the zigzag stitch, the needle positions create smooth points and corners in appliqué.

Needle position options vary from machine to machine. There are three basic needle positions: left (L), center (C), and right (R). Many machines offer five or more needle positions. These positions can have names like left, near left, near right, and right, or may be numbered L1, L2 and R1, R2.

On some brands of machines, the needle positions are part of the stitch selection. The machine might have three different straight stitch patterns, each one in a different needle position. A few machines are in a permanent center or left needle position. Occasionally, a machine has a selection of needle positions in only straight stitch, with the other stitches permanently locked in center position. Then there are machines that have variable needle positions in every stitch.

ZIGZAG STITCH

The zigzag stitch is the second most frequently used stitch. There are three variables for the zigzag stitch: stitch length, needle position, and stitch width. (Also, there can be three levels to control the stitch length.)

It is important to know the maximum and minimum stitch length of your sewing machine. Some machines have a separate stitch selection for zigzag, and another one for satin stitch.

Remember satin stitch is a form of zigzag, but the stitch length settings for satin stitch are very short, usually under .5 on the metric scale. Frequently, the delicate stitch length adjustments required for satin stitch are part of a second scale, called density control, or balance control. This scale affects the stitches under .5 in length.

Determine the possible needle positions. On some brands of machines, the needle positions are part of the stitch selection. The machine might have three different zigzag patterns, each one in a different needle position. It is also important to know the maximum and minimum stitch width. As in the straight stitch, the scale can be metric or an independent scale.

STITCH WIDTH

Metric scale (millimeters). The metric scale is common on new machines and is the scale I use throughout the book. It is a logical system based on millimeters. (Just remember, $1/4$" equals about 6 millimeters.) The number on the dial indicates the width of each stitch when sewn on two layers of medium weight cotton fabric. For example:

1.0 means that each stitch is 1 millimeter in width.

2.0 means each stitch is 2 millimeters in width.

3.0 means each stitch is 3 millimeters in width or $1/8$" inch wide.

4.0 means each stitch is 4 millimeters in width.

6.0 means each stitch is 6 millimeters or $1/4$" wide.

9.0 means each stitch is 9 millimeters or $3/8$" wide.

Independent scales. Some machines do not use a metric scale

for stitch width. Some use a numbered system; others a series of pictures. This can make it difficult to translate generic directions to your machine. To correlate your machine's scale to a metric scale may require a little work. First, I recommend checking in the owner's manual. The manual may explain how the scale relates to metrics. If you can't find that information, make a stitch width sample.

Sew A Sample

STITCH WIDTH SAMPLE

Supplies

• 6" x 3" piece of light-colored cotton broadcloth

• 1 piece of typing paper

Machine Setup

Thread the machine with contrasting thread in the bobbin and in the needle. Mismatched thread makes it easier to see the individual stitches.

1 This sample is like the one used for stitch length on page 4. It's a 6" x 3" piece of fabric backed with typing paper. Mark one inch intervals on the right side of the fabric.

2 Set the machine for a different stitch width in each inch section, then measure the width of the stitches to determine the stitch width in metrics.

3 Set the machine for a stitch length of one (1.0) and the widest stitch width.

4 Sew 1" at this setting. Write the stitch width on the fabric next to this portion of the stitching.

5 Continue to adjust the stitch width and record the stitch width number.

6 Remove the sample from the machine and use a metric ruler to measure the stitch width in each marked inch.

AUTOMATIC OR DECORATIVE STITCHES

The techniques in this book mostly use three basic groups of stitches: blind stitches, hand duplication stitches, and compact or satin stitches. Each group has separate uses.

BLIND STITCHES

Blind stitches, including blindhem or overlock stitches, replace hand blind stitches. They are a frequent choice for appliqué and binding. Blind stitches have two parts, a line of straight stitching divided by an occasional zigzag. See Fig. 1-2 for illustrations of possible blind stitches. Notice that some of the stitches zig to the left, others to

The Woven Basket block from my *Floral Urns* quilt shows the use of automatic stitches.

the right. There are also differences in how many straight stitches divide the zigzags.

DUPLICATION OF HAND STITCHES

This group includes the buttonhole stitch, feather and fly stitch, and stem stitches. These stitches look like traditional hand embroidery stitches of the same name. Hand duplication stitches are the perfect counterpart to appliqué and broderie perse.

Buttonhole stitch. This is not the satin stitch used to make functional buttonholes, but a stitch that duplicates hand buttonhole stitching (see Fig. 1-3). This stitch has at least three other names, point de Paris, pin stitch, and single hem stitch. No matter the name, the basic elements of the stitch are the same. Like blind stitches, it has two parts, a line of straight stitches divided by a zigzag. However, the zigzag is not feeding forward. Compare Fig. 1-3 (buttonhole illustrations) to Fig. 1-2 (blind stitch illustrations). Notice the difference in the zigzag portion? True buttonhole

stitch has a closed zigzag. Also note the zigzag stitch is perpendicular to the straight stitch line. Only perpendicular stitches are capable of turning sharp corners. The buttonhole stitches with angled zigzags have limited use.

There are two basic buttonhole stitches: single-stitched buttonhole and multiple-stitched buttonhole. On some machines the buttonhole stitch is a forward moving stitch, and every stitch is a single line of thread. On other machines the fabric moves forward and backward so every stitch is oversewn at least two times. Multiple stitched buttonhole looks thicker, more like hand-stitched appliqué sewn with embroidery floss. Although thinner, the single stitched buttonhole is easier to control on corners and curves.

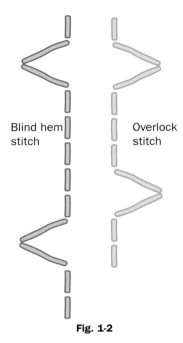

Blind hem stitch   Overlock stitch

Fig. 1-2

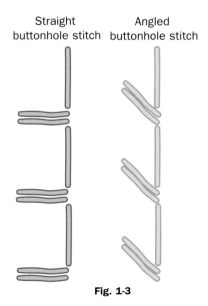

Straight buttonhole stitch   Angled buttonhole stitch

Fig. 1-3

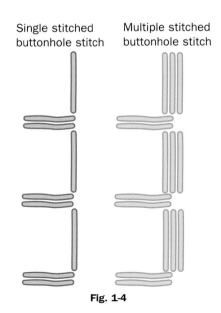

Single stitched buttonhole stitch   Multiple stitched buttonhole stitch

Fig. 1-4

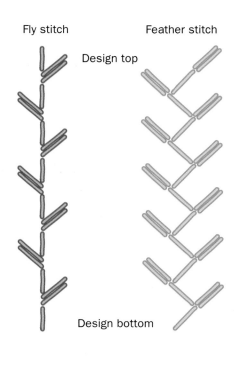

Fly stitch　　　Feather stitch

Design top

Design bottom

Fig. 1-5

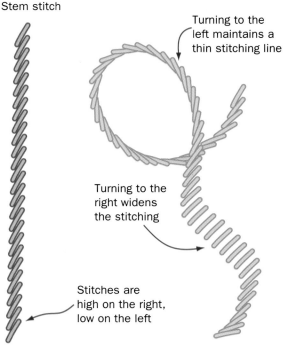

Stem stitch

Turning to the left maintains a thin stitching line

Turning to the right widens the stitching

Stitches are high on the right, low on the left

Fig. 1-6

Feather and fly stitches.
Feather stitch has the branched look of a true feather stitch. Fly stitch has very similar branches, but the fly stitch has a straight stitch spine, while the feather stitch has a zigzag base. In true fly stitch, the branches always are in pairs. Frequently machine fly stitches have single alternating branches. The fly stitch with its straight spine is the most versatile. It is the easiest to control on corners and curves. Check your machine for variations of feather and fly stitches. For example, the Pfaff Creative 7550 has a great pattern for a fly stitch leaf, pattern number 126.

Stem stitch. This stitch is a straight stitch variation. The machine guides the fabric forward and backward to form an angled line of stitches that resemble the hand stem stitch. Some machines have a single stitched stem, while others have a multiple stitched stem. The multiple stitched stem is

heavier and looks more like hand embroidery. Both stitches work equally well.

COMPACT OR DECORATIVE STITCHES

These stitches are satin stitch based, and use a short stitch length

to get smooth, filled-in designs. In appliqué these stitches add texture to the fabrics. They can replace tiny portions of appliqué that are just too small to cut from fabric. There are dozens of possible patterns. I consistently use about four patterns: daisy petals, circles, half circles, and leaf patterns.

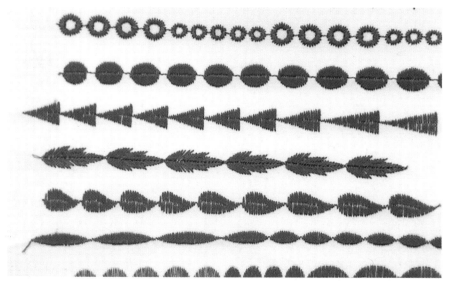

A selection of compact stitches suitable for embellishing appliqué. These stitches can be substituted for small pieces of appliqué, or used as added embroidery.

COMPUTERIZED SEWING MACHINE FEATURES

The new computerized machines have many extras not available on older machines. Don't worry if your machine doesn't fit this category. The computer features make things easier, but aren't a prerequisite for most of the techniques in this book. The following features are the most useful for appliqué.

SINGLE PATTERN

This feature allows the machine to make one complete pattern and stop. When selected, the machine begins and ends with a securing knot. A companion to single pattern is pattern begin. This ensures starting at the true beginning of the pattern.

MIRROR IMAGING

This feature changes the stitching direction of the pattern. There are both lateral and axial imaging.

❑ Lateral imaging flips the pattern right to left. For example, a basic buttonhole stitch is usually straight stitches on the left, and zigs to the right. With lateral imaging engaged, the pattern straight stitches on the right and zigs to the left.

❑ Axial imaging makes the end of the pattern the beginning, and works only on one-way designs. Take for example the leaf stitch in Fig. 1-7. The regular stitch starts at the base of the leaf and stitches toward the point. With axial imaging engaged, the stitching starts at the point and stitches toward the base.

Lateral mirror imaging is by far the most common. If you confuse lateral and axial imaging, you have to remember only one term, lateral. I remember what lateral imaging does because lateral starts with an "L" like left, and lateral flips left for right. By default, I then know what axial is.

For a little more fun, use lateral and axial imaging on the same stitch. It boggles the mind! Fig. 1-7 shows the same pattern in the four possibilities.

 **Caution**

Even if a machine has lateral and axial imaging, these features may not function with every stitch.

DOUBLE NEEDLE

The double needle feature automatically reduces the stitch width of every pattern to prevent breaking needles when using double or twin needles. Think of it this way: the feature cuts the stitch width in half and can have a lot more uses than just double needle work. It helps maintain a uniform stitch width throughout a project and helps in tapering the zigzag width.

AUTO KNOT

This feature makes a secure knot at the beginning and end of every line of stitching, without your using the reverse button. Typically, this knot is a "pigtail" knot. That means a neat, discreet knot that requires careful handling of the thread tails.

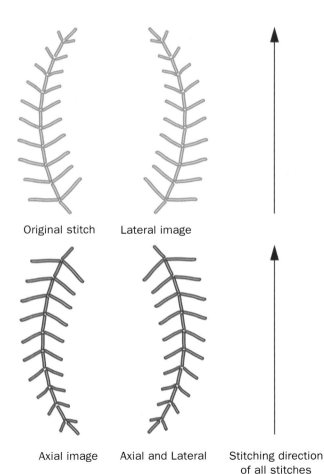

Original stitch   Lateral image

Axial image   Axial and Lateral   Stitching direction of all stitches

Fig. 1-7

Machine Savvy

WHAT IS A "PIGTAIL" KNOT?

The term *pigtail* refers to the way the knot looks on the wrong side of the fabric. The knot is formed by the twisting of the needle and bobbin threads, when the machine stitches up and down in one spot. The top thread wraps around the bobbin thread and looks like a pig's corkscrew tail. To use a pigtail knot, clip the needle thread close to the fabric, then tug on the bobbin thread to pull any remaining wisps of top thread to the wrong side of the work. Cut the bobbin thread tail at least $1/8$" to $1/4$" away from the knot to keep the knot intact.

PROGRAMMABLE STITCHES

If you're lucky enough to own the newest and best, you know that many of these machines are programmable to create an unbelievable array of stitches. Some machines have built in programs that allow the freedom of designing stitches. A few machines interface with a laptop computer. You no longer have to "make do" with the standard machine stitches. Now you are the designer and programmer and can customize your machine's stitches to fit your demands.

Personally, I'm hooked. I can't imagine serious sewing without these great features.

Presser Feet

CHAPTER 2 FOCUSES ON the sewing machine presser feet used throughout the book. Many of the techniques in this book depend on using specialized presser feet. This chapter lists, and gives a brief description of, the feet used to make the samples in this book.

Don't rush out and buy every foot listed! For many techniques two or more feet can produce the same results. The technique directions give a list of suitable feet with directions for their use.

Most of these feet are available from your sewing machine dealer or as a generic foot through mail order sewing notions catalogs. I have tried to choose feet that are easily obtainable for any brand of machine. However, these feet are only representative of what you might need. What suits your needs or your specific brand might look different and have a different number. Talk to your dealer about what

you want to do, and let your dealer recommend the appropriate foot. If your dealer can't help you, then look for the generic feet listed in mail order sewing notions catalogs.

Machine Savvy

WHAT ARE GENERIC FEET?

The term *generic* means the foot wasn't manufactured for only a specific brand of sewing machine. It will fit many machines. Generic feet

are available through mail order catalogs and from fabric and quilt stores. They come in three basic styles: high shank, low shank, and snap on. This refers to the way the foot attaches to the machine. But, high shank, low shank, and snap on styles are not the only way feet attach to the machine—there are also slant shanks, and brand-specific feet like those made for Bernina machines. It is important that you know what style shank is on your machine before buying generic presser feet.

BASIC FEET

Regular zigzag foot. This is the basic foot that comes as a standard accessory with all zigzag machines.

Zipper foot. This basic foot frequently is a standard accessory with most machines. Its original purpose is sewing in zippers.

Standard embroidery foot. The embroidery foot can be plastic or metal. The foot looks like a regular zigzag foot with the exception of the sole underneath. The sole of the foot has a wide groove to allow the even feeding of embroidery stitches.

Top   Underside

Underside

Top   Underside

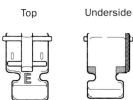

Top   Underside

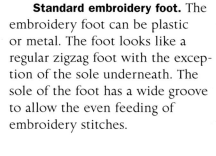

Underside

Underside

Top   Underside

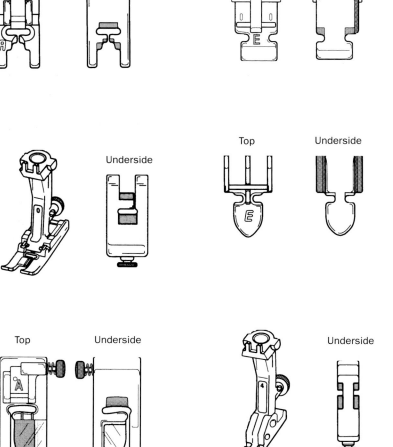

Underside

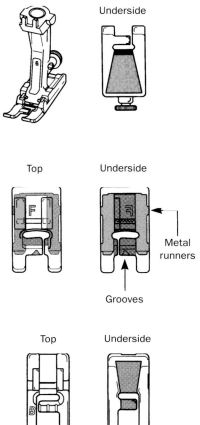

Metal runners

Grooves

Top   Underside

FEET WITH GUIDES

Open toe embroidery foot or no-bridge embroidery foot. This is the single most important foot for machine appliqué. This foot is a modification of the standard embroidery foot. Removing the bridge between the toes of the foot gives a clear view of the needle and fabric edge. This foot is an extra accessory for every brand of machine. It is available as a brand name foot or a generic foot.

Underside

These feet are all notable for the metal or plastic blade on the foot. The blade is used to guide the fabric with an exact and uniform placement under the foot. These feet may or may not come with your machine. There are three styles:

1 Feet that can guide only to the right or only to the left of an edge

2 Feet that can guide on either side of an edge

3 Feet with loops or slots for guiding trims

The most usable of the feet is the edge-joining foot that guides fabric on either side of the guide. The type of feet that fit in this category are:

❑ Overlock foot

❑ Blindhem foot—usually guides right side of an edge

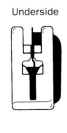

Underside

Top   Underside

❑ Edgestitch foot (can be obtained as generic)—usually guides right side of an edge

❑ Satin-edge/Topstitch foot (can be obtained as generic)—usually guides right side of an edge

Top   Underside

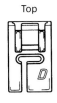

Top   Underside

❑ Edge-joining foot (can be obtained as generic)—guides on either side

❑ Sequin/Ribbon foot (can be obtained as generic)—has a loop guide

FEET WITH GROOVES

This group of feet have a common prominent feature: they have deep grooves on the underside of the foot. On most of the feet the grooves serve as a guide for heavy fabric or as a tunnel for a filler thread. These feet may or may not come with your machine. The type of feet that fit in this category are:

Pintuck foot. Three, five, seven, or nine groove foot. The numbers of grooves denote the size of the grooves. The more grooves on a foot, the smaller the grooves (can be obtained as generic).

Top   Underside

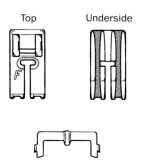

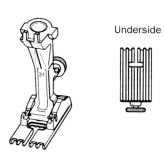

Underside

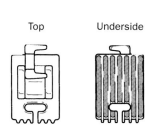

Top   Underside

Buttonhole foot. This is a basic buttonhole foot, and usually doesn't measure the buttonhole length. This foot has two grooves directly behind the needle opening to guide the channels of the satin stitch.

Top   Underside

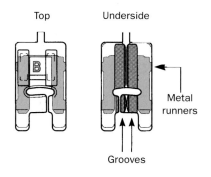

Metal runners

Grooves

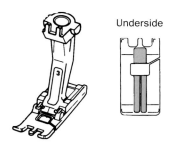

Underside

Piping, beading, or welting foot. The piping or welting foot makes piping or welting for garment construction or upholstery. The beading foot attaches strands or strings of beads. All these feet come in different sizes depending on the intended use (can be obtained as generic).

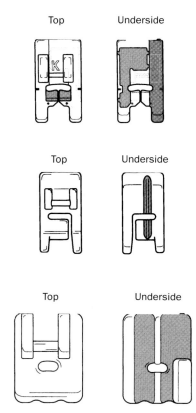

Top   Underside

Top   Underside

Top   Underside

Bulky fabric foot or knit edge foot. These feet have an uneven base to help smoothly feed the thickness of the heavy fabric layers. The foot is also called a Compensating foot. Some feet are

Underside

thin on the right side of the foot and thick on the left side; other feet have the opposite arrangement. Both styles of feet are useful for quiltmaking. Some bulky fabric feet have full width zigzag needle openings. Other styles of feet have straight stitch or reduced width zigzag needle openings. Bernina machines have two versions of this foot. My favorite is called the heavy piping foot, number 38.

Appliqué foot. This foot has a single narrow groove directly behind the needle opening.

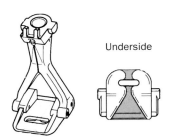

Underside

These feet are representative of what you need to duplicate the techniques in this book. The specific brand that you require might look different from these and have a different number. Talk to your dealer about what you want the foot to do, or for what purpose you want to use this foot. Your dealer should be able to recommend the appropriate foot. If your dealer can't help you, look for the generic feet listed in mail order sewing notions catalogs.

ASSORTED ACCESSORIES

There are a number of supplies and accessories that can make the sewing experience more enjoyable.

Extra bobbin case. Many novelty threads require a second bobbin case because novelty threads require bobbin tension adjustments. The extra case replaces your regular bobbin case. This allows adjustments to the bobbin tension without worrying about affecting the machine's normal sewing. Simply use the first bobbin case for regular sewing and use the extra case exclusively for decorative threads.

This accessory is really a machine part. Depending on the brand of machine, there may be a special bobbin case available or you can buy a second regular bobbin case. This accessory is available only on machines that have a removable bobbin case. Machines with a drop-in bobbin feature cannot obtain an extra bobbin case.

Plexiglas table extension. The Plexiglas table extension for the free arm machine is a "gem" of a table. It fits the free arm of the sewing machine and increases the working space to the left, front, and back of the presser foot. The larger sewing surface results in straighter and more even stitching that is easier to guide. In addition, it's better for your back and arms.

Part Two

Fabric Preparation for Appliqué

Floral Urns **quilt by Debra Wagner.**

CHAPTER 3

Awesome Appliqués

THE SEWING MACHINE is capable of making breathtakingly detailed appliqués in a fraction of the time required by hand. Delicate corners, sharp points, and complex shapes are a piece of cake by machine. Machine appliqué is always smooth and flat, with perfectly even stitches that would take a hand stitcher years to master. Although stitches look similar to those used in handwork, machine appliqué is fundamentally different from hand appliqué. The machine stitch always requires two threads, and the needle must pierce the top of the appliqué. In hand appliqué you use one thread and slip it invisibly in and out of the seam allowance. After twenty years of machine embroidery and appliqué, I am convinced that machine appliqué should not try to be a replacement for needle-turned hand appliqué. Rather, machine appliqué has its own look, rules, and techniques that make use of the machine's special features.

This chapter covers supplies and basic information for all appliqué methods plus techniques for preparing the appliqué pieces for turned-edge appliqué, and for preparing the appliqué pieces for raw-edge appliqué, including broderie perse. For ways to stitch appliqué to the background fabric, see Part III (starting on page 49).

GENERAL APPLIQUÉ SUPPLIES

- Fabrics
- Starch
- Freezer paper
- Sharp embroidery scissors
- Gluestick
- Basic thread for appliqué
- Machine needles
- Open toe or no-bridge embroidery foot
- Hemostat

Fabrics. I recommend 100% cotton broadcloth for the appliqués and background blocks.

Hot Tip

Print fabrics conceal the stitching while solids accentuate it.

Starch. Use heavy spray starch in aerosol cans or pump bottles for small pieces. Use liquid starch that requires diluting with water for fabric yardage. For more information, read the section on Basic Fabric Preparation on this page.

Freezer paper. Use any brand of plastic or polyethylene-coated freezer paper.

Gluestick. I recommend any brand that is non-permanent. Keep the gluestick in the freezer when not in use. Frozen gluestick is easier

to handle; freezing makes the glue less gooey and it lasts longer.

Basic thread for appliqué. Basic appliqué thread makes the least conspicuous stitches. That's why I don't recommend you use poly/cotton or any other kind of sewing thread. There are two choices for appliqué thread: invisible machine quilting thread, or 100% cotton machine embroidery thread (size 50, 60, or 80). The thread color matches the fabrics or is a shade darker. As a rule of thumb, a darker colored thread shows less than a lighter shade.

Machine Savvy

WHAT DO THE THREAD NUMBERS MEAN?

The higher the thread number, the finer the thread (which, of course, is just the opposite of needles where the higher the number, the thicker the needle). Thread size 80 or 100 is very fine, usually used for appliqué, French hand sewing, or darning. With fine thread use a 65/9 or 70/10 needle. Finer threads and needles result in smaller stitches and needle holes.

Machine needles. Use size 65/9 or 70/10 regular machine needles for size 50, 60, or 80 machine embroidery threads. Use size 80/12 regular machine needle for size 30 machine embroidery thread.

Hemostat. This small surgical instrument is a cross between tweezers and pliers. Its small shape makes it perfect to work in tiny corners and points of appliqué. It helps turn edges and holds the pieces in place when stitching.

BASIC FABRIC PREPARATION

STARCHING THE APPLIQUÉ FABRICS

Some appliqué pieces require starching prior to use. Starched fabric is easier to handle and stitch. A good coat of starch can be the secret to great, trouble-free appliquéing.

Starching small pieces. To starch small pieces of fabric use spray starch in an aerosol can or pump bottle. Spray starch is best for small pieces. To use spray starch, mist the fabric with a coat of starch. Wait a moment to let the starch penetrate the fabric. Press until dry with an iron on the cotton setting. Do not use steam. Use a single application for light starch. Repeat the process at least three times for heavy starch. Do not use this method for yardage.

Starching yardage. To starch yardage, use a plant mister to apply the starch, then permit the fabric to air-dry. Hang the dry, unstarched yardage on a clothesline or in a shower stall. Mix starch and water to obtain the correct intensity of starch. For light starch use a mixture of 25% liquid starch to 75% water. For heavy starch use a mixture of 50% water to 50% liquid starch. Spray on the mixture soaking the fabric with the starch. Allow the fabric hang until dry. Steam press to remove any wrinkles. Store any excess starch mixture in the refrigerator to keep it fresh.

STABILIZING THE BACKGROUND FABRIC

Back the background fabric with freezer paper. Freezer paper makes fabric easier to guide, and improves stitch appearance. Tension and stitch length and width adjustments are easier with a freezer paper backing. Place the poly-coated side of the freezer paper against the wrong side of the fabric and press. Use an iron at the cotton setting. Do not use steam. Move the iron slowly to adhere paper to fabric. There is no right or wrong way to press these pieces, although I usually press from the paper side.

Hot Tip

Speed up the pressing time and improve the adherence of the freezer paper by warming up the fabric before applying the paper. Simply press the fabric and immediately place the freezer paper in place.

Sewing Savvy

When cutting your fabrics, allow at least 1" seam allowances on the background fabrics. Machine appliqué causes some fabric distortion. Large seam allowances compensate for the problem. Cut the block to the correct size after completing the appliqué and embroidery.

MARKING THE PATTERN AND POSITIONING THE APPLIQUÉ PIECES

This section describes a number of traditional methods used to position appliqué pieces on the background. Choose any technique. The method is not as important as the results. The pattern marking method chosen should allow *accurate* and easy placement of all the pieces. I have had some bad experiences and

have my favorite methods when it comes to positioning appliqués.

What can go wrong when marking the appliqué pattern? The most common method to mark the appliqué pattern is to mark the pattern on the background fabric using a fabric marker. This method is the most straightforward, but it

has inherent problems, especially with detailed multi-layered designs like flowers (see Fig. 3-1). The first couple of pieces in the flower cover the markings for the remaining pieces in that flower (see Fig. 3-2). The more pieces, the more room for errors. Frequently, pattern directions suggest placing

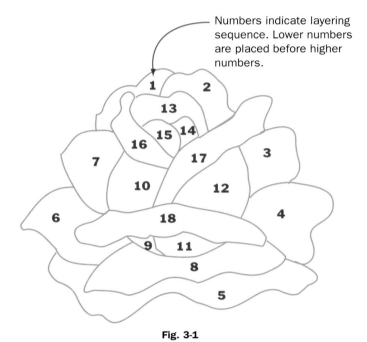

Numbers indicate layering sequence. Lower numbers are placed before higher numbers.

Fig. 3-1

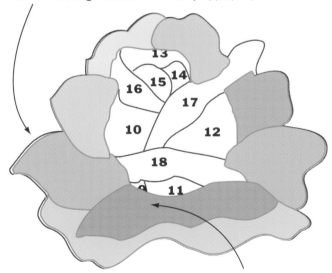

Pattern lines might not be covered by appliqué pieces.

Lower numbered pieces may obscure the placement lines of higher numbered pieces.

Fig. 3-2

the complex pieces by guess or
"by eye." This can be tricky. The
appliqué can become so distorted
that the last pieces aren't covering
all the raw edges of the first
pieces. It is easy to "eye" the location of simple appliqués, but many
patterns are just too complex to
guess at the location of the pieces.
If you want the block to look *just
like* the pattern, guessing doesn't
always give that result.

I have two favorite methods
for marking appliqué patterns.
I routinely use these non-marking
methods with excellent results.
Most often I use a combination of
both techniques. I use a light box
for the simple sections of the
block, and a sheet of acetate for
the more complex sections. The
light box is easiest; the acetate
sheet, the most accurate.

Light box method. Use a light
box to place simple appliqués.
Place a clear line drawing of the
pattern on the light box. Center
the background fabric over the
pattern. The drawing shows
through the fabric and serves as a
placement guide for the pieces.

 **Caution**

**This method doesn't work
well on multi-layered appliqué.
Multiple layers of appliqué
obscure the pattern lines.**

Acetate sheet method. Use
an acetate sheet to place complex
appliqués. I learned this wonderful
method from the pattern directions for *Curiosity* patterns.
(*Curiosity* puts out a wide range of
gorgeous floral appliqué patterns,
available at your local quilt store.)
Their method of appliqué placement is the best I've used for complex, multi-layered appliqué. They
recommend drawing the pattern
on a sheet of acetate. Place the

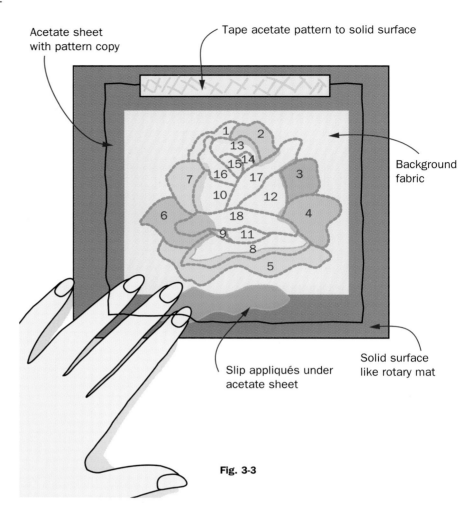

Acetate sheet
with pattern copy

Tape acetate pattern to solid surface

Background
fabric

Slip appliqués under
acetate sheet

Solid surface
like rotary mat

Fig. 3-3

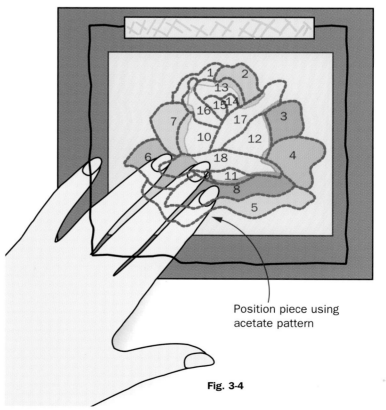

Position piece using
acetate pattern

Fig. 3-4

acetate sheet over the background fabric. Position the appliqué pieces by slipping them between the acetate and background fabric. This assures accurate placement on even the most complex designs.

 Hot Tip

Jan Dalton of *Curiosity* told me about a great way to transfer patterns to the acetate. She suggests using a copy machine and the special acetate sheets made for use with the copy machine.

Copy machines require a special type of acetate that does not melt on the heated rollers. The correct type of acetate (used to make transparencies) is available at art, hobby, or office supply stores. When using a copy machine to transfer the pattern to the acetate, check the copy against the original to be sure it's not distorted.

When large designs do not fit on a single sheet of acetate, run the design on a number of sheets. Then, using the original pattern as a guide, tape the sheets together with invisible tape to form a single pattern sheet. The method is neat and easy. Thanks, Jan!

DETERMINING THE APPLIQUÉ LAYERS

Many appliqués are layers of pieces stacked one on top of another, much like a dimensional sculpture. The layering affects the cutting and stitching of pieces. Usually, a number on the pattern distinguishes the individual appliqué pieces

and how the pieces relate to each other. The lower numbered pieces fall partially behind the high numbered pieces. Though many designers pre-number the simple appliqué patterns, frequently, complex patterns aren't numbered. Don't panic. There are many possible correct sequences for each pattern. When faced with a pattern without numbers, you can determine an appropriate layering sequence. It helps to think in 3-D.

It is safe to assume the layering sequence is stems, leaves, flowers, buds, calyxes. As a simple example, see the four piece tulip in Fig. 3-5. The stem is under the tulip. The stem is #1. The leaves cover the stem and are #2. The center petal of the tulip is behind the two outer petals. The center petal is #3, with the two outer petals #4.

Two cardinal rules to layering an appliqué are: 1. *Never* butt two appliqué edges together. This results in double stitching lines. 2. The lower numbered pieces must extend under the higher numbered pieces.

To conform to the rules, add an extra tab or extension of fabric to every appliqué piece that touches a higher numbered piece. In Figure 3-6, the stem and center petal have a 1/4" extension on the edges that touch the outer petals. This extension is rarely marked on the appliqué pattern; it would make the pattern too confusing to read. It is up to you to add the extensions to the correct edges. For the beginner, I suggest making a duplicate of the pattern by tracing or using a copy machine to

copy the original pattern. Using the pattern copy, mark the extensions. Lightly draw and shade in the extensions using a soft lead pencil.

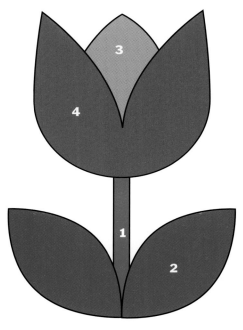

Fig. 3-5

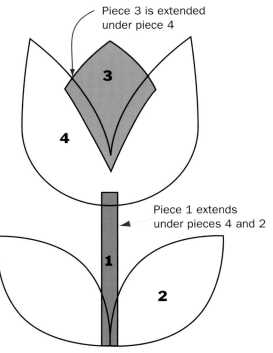

Piece 3 is extended under piece 4

Piece 1 extends under pieces 4 and 2

Fig. 3-6

HOW TO DETERMINE THE APPLIQUÉ LAYERS

1 Place the appliqué pieces in proper order on the background following. Start with #1 and layer the pieces in numerical sequence.

2 Use gluestick to hold the appliqué layers in place before fusing them or stitching them in place.

3 All the appliqué pieces may be layered or pre-placed before you start to stitch, or you can layer and stitch each piece before placing the next piece. Either method is successful and has advantages when used with the appropriate appliqué method.

Raw-edge method. With the raw-edge method of appliqué, layer all the pieces before stitching. This is fast and reduces the chances of stitching on appliqué edges that fall under other pieces. With raw-edge appliqué methods, any line of stitching that falls under another appliqué piece becomes extremely obvious and can spoil the look of the appliqué.

Pre-placed appliqué does have one drawback: it is hard to knot the thread inconspicuously. Higher numbered appliqué pieces won't conceal the knots on the lower numbered pieces. Careful knotting is a requirement at both the beginning and end of every stitching line.

Turned-edge method. When using turned-edge appliqué, layer and stitch each piece before placing the next piece. This method conceals the thread knots under other pieces of appliqué and adds strength to the stitching.

CHAPTER 4
Turned-Edge Appliqué Methods

GREAT TURNED-EDGES without freezer paper? Flawless and fast stems, vines, and woven baskets using two straight pins? Perfect $1/8"$ stems and vines using the pintuck foot? These techniques and more are part of this chapter, including how to prepare turned-edge appliqué pieces; for stitching techniques, see Chapter 6.

Turned-edge appliqué is the most common form of appliqué. The turned seam allowances give the appliqué a slight dimensional appearance. Woven baskets, vines, and stems look better when done with turned-edge methods.

TURNED-EDGE MACHINE APPLIQUÉ

For machine appliqué, the seam allowance edge must be turned prior to starting the appliqué. As a devotee of needle-turned hand appliqué, I used to find this preparatory step distasteful. I had

trouble finding a basic method of turning edges that was as enjoyable as doing needle-turn appliqué. I liked the neat crisp results I achieved using freezer paper, but *loathed* having to spend time and patience removing the paper from the back of each piece. Cutting the background or soaking away the paper seemed an impossible task on complex blocks.

Everything changed when I found HTC Rinse Away stabilizer. I substitute Rinse Away for freezer paper. Rinse Away has the thickness of lightweight cardboard. It makes a perfect template for turning seam allowances. Rinse

Away combined with gluestick gives the same accurate results as freezer paper *without* having to remove it from the back of the appliqué piece. Rinse Away remains in the appliqué and disintegrates when the quilt is washed. It leaves behind only a light web of fibers. The fiber web doesn't negatively affect the appliqué. Actually, the extra web of fibers enhances the dimensional quality of the finished piece. In addition, the web of white fibers solves the problem of shadowing when stitching light fabrics over dark. This allows you to place light-colored appliqué pieces over darker colors without a hint of color showing through.

I would like to think that everyone, including "hand appliquérs," will love my method of turning edges. Yet, I know there are dozens of other techniques for turning the seam allowances; you may already have a favorite way that gives great results. The method used to turn the edge is not important. Only the results count. The appliqué pieces should be accurate, with smooth curves and sharp points.

Sew A Sample

TURNED-EDGE APPLIQUÉ SAMPLE

Supplies

• Cotton fabrics, lightly starched and pressed for the appliqué

• Prepared block background, prepared according to basic appliqué instructions on page 20.

• Pigma 01 pen or other fine line permanent pen

• Gluestick

• Circle template available from office supply stores

• Lightweight cardboard, e.g., a manila folder

• HTC Rinse Away stabilizer. This is a water-soluble stabilizer.

The sample I made to experiment with using Rinse Away in appliqués.

HTC Rinse Away stabilizer looks and acts much like a medium-weight non-woven interfacing with one large exception—it disintegrates in water. As far as I know, there is no current substitute for this brand name product. My many thanks to Debbie Casteel for helping me find this great product!

PAPER-BACKED APPLIQUÉ USING RINSE AWAY

Paper-backed appliqué turns the seam allowances over a paper template. In my technique Rinse Away replaces the paper used in traditional methods. Paper-backed appliqué results in a neatly turned edge that is smooth, stable, and easy to stitch. The method is suitable for most pattern pieces, although tiny or detailed pieces might get distorted. Use the turned-edge method for "gentle" corners and curved designs that have a limited number of sharp

points or deep curves. The most successful corners are at least 45° wide, and individual pieces should be larger than a dime. Fig. 4-1 shows the types of design features that are difficult for turned-edge appliqué.

 Hot Tip

On complex multi-layered appliqué, I number every template according to the layering sequence. As I trace the template onto the Rinse Away, I number the Rinse Away template. The numbers mark the location on the block and help to keep track of the dozens of small templates and appliqué pieces.

BONDING LAYERS OF RINSE AWAY

The paper-backed method of turning edges uses a double layer of Rinse Away. Two layers of Rinse Away are equal in thickness to a manila file folder. The thickness

makes it *extremely* easy to turn the seam allowance. Bonding together the layers of Rinse Away gives a firm edge.

To bond, activate the water soluble properties of Rinse Away with water, to act as a glue holding the pieces together. Using a plant mister filled with water, mist two pieces of Rinse Away until damp. Wait a minute then place the damp sides of the two pieces together. Place the pieces on the ironing board and cover with a piece of muslin. Using an iron on the cotton setting, press until the layers of Rinse Away have dried.

 Caution

Never let the iron touch damp Rinse Away! It leaves a terrible, sticky, burnt mess.

TIPS ON PRESSING RINSE AWAY

❑ To remove Rinse Away from an iron, wait till the iron cools, then wash the soleplate of the iron with terrycloth moistened with *hot* water. Robbie Fanning suggests cleaning off Rinse Away by sliding the warm iron on an unscented Bounce dryer sheet.

❑ Reduce the time spent pressing the Rinse Away with a little planning. Press the layers for a few minutes, just enough to start the drying process. Remove the press cloth and let the Rinse Away air dry on the ironing board. It requires more time for the layers to dry, but leaves you free to prepare other parts of the appliqué.

❑ To get a smooth flat bond, the entire Rinse Away piece should fit on the ironing board. Keep the size under

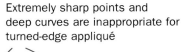
Extremely sharp points and deep curves are inappropriate for turned-edge appliqué

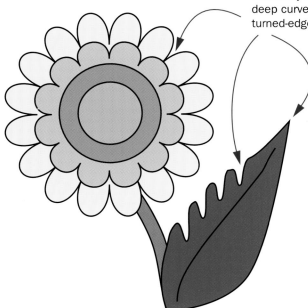
Fig. 4-1

12" X 22". Bonded Rinse Away is stiff and difficult to store. Prepare pieces only as needed.

MAKING RINSE AWAY TEMPLATES

1 To make templates, trace individual pieces onto the Rinse Away. Use a fine line pencil or Pigma pen. Do not add seam allowances to the pieces. Trace the pieces from the reverse side of the pattern. I suggest using a dotted line to mark the edges that will be overlapped by other appliqué pieces. Do not turn the seam allowances on these edges.

2 Mark every Rinse Away piece with its template number.

 Sewing Savvy

Draw the template pattern pieces from the wrong side to ensure the marking is not visible through the appliqué pieces. Don't invert the pattern pieces. It is important to keep track of the wrong side of the pattern pieces. Inverted templates cause reversed pieces. If you inverted all the templates, it would be acceptable, because it would reverse the entire design. But we all know what happens, only a piece or two ends up wrong and throws off the whole design.

3 Cut out the template pieces on the marked line.

4 Place a dab of gluestick on the right (unmarked) side of the Rinse Away template and adhere it to the wrong side of the appliqué fabric. Cut out the appliqué fabric adding a

scant ¼" seam allowance around the template.

TURNING SEAM ALLOWANCES ON CORNERED AND CURVED APPLIQUÉ PIECES

The next steps turn the seam allowances and secure them in place with gluestick. Turning edges requires corner and curve skills. Neat curves and corners are the hallmark of good appliqué. There are two curves, the inside curve and the outside curve. Corners are classified by the width and the directions in which they point. There are four types of corners. The wide corners are 90° or greater and can be inside or outside points. The narrow or fine corners are less than 90° and can be inside or outside points.

 **Sew A Sample**

SAMPLE FOR TURNING BASIC CORNERS AND CURVES

The three practice pieces suggested here explain how to turn the basic corners and curves. You will also use these samples for the stitching sample in the next section.

For each of the three samples, begin with these basic instructions:

1 Cut out the templates from Rinse Away. For the sample, you may cut the templates from manila file folders. (For the sample, leave the manila template in the appliqué. In an actual appliqué, the manila file folder would cause

problems and would have to be removed prior to stitching the appliqué.)

2 Using gluestick, glue the templates to the wrong side of the fabric.

3 Cut out the appliqué fabric adding a scant ¼" seam allowance. Move on to separate instructions for each sample, as follows.

90°-OR-GREATER INSIDE AND OUTSIDE CORNERS

1 On the inside corners, make a single clip toward the inside corner. The clip should stop a thread or two from the exact corner (see Fig. 4-2).

2 Apply gluestick to the wrong side of seam allowances and edges of one of the points. Apply gluestick on a flat surface for better coverage. Place scrap paper under the appliqué when applying the gluestick. It keeps the work area clean.

3 Start at the inside corner. The seam allowance splits at the clips (see Fig. 4-3).

With your fingertips, fold the seam allowances over the template. Make sure the seam allowance "hugs" the inside corner. Pinch and hold the seam allowance in place until the glue holds.

⬟ **Hot Tip**

A hemostat works well for catching and turning tiny seam allowances.

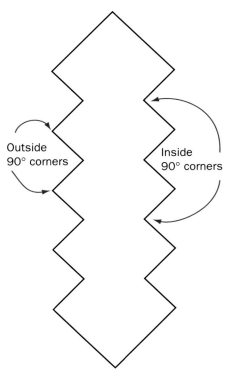

Outside 90° corners

Inside 90° corners

Fig. 4-2   Pattern provided is 50% of full size. Enlarge on a photocopy machine or transfer from ½" to 1" grid to obtain full-size pattern.

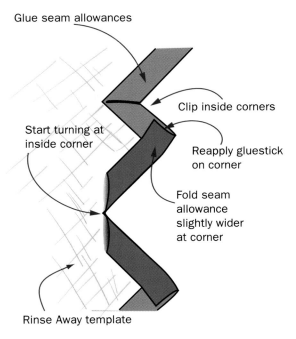

Glue seam allowances

Clip inside corners

Start turning at inside corner

Reapply gluestick on corner

Fold seam allowance slightly wider at corner

Rinse Away template

Fig. 4-3

4 Turn the seam allowance over the glued edge working towards the outside corner. At the very point, fold the seam allowance over the corner. When folding seam allowance onto seam allowance fold a slightly wider allowance. This helps conceal the seam allowance under the point of the corner.

5 Place another dot of gluestick on the turned seam allowance. This helps hold the seam allowance on the second side of the corner.

6 Turn the second seam allowance over the point of the corner. Make sure the second fold is not visible from the right side of the appliqué.

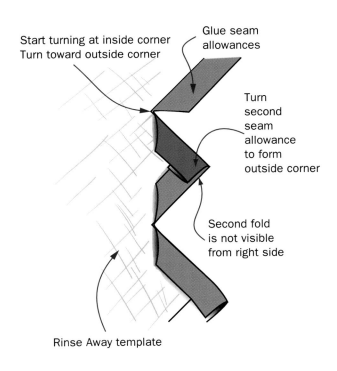

Start turning at inside corner
Turn toward outside corner

Glue seam allowances

Turn second seam allowance to form outside corner

Second fold is not visible from right side

Rinse Away template

Fig. 4-4

LESS-THAN-90° INSIDE AND OUTSIDE CORNERS

Follow the previous directions until the turning of the second side of the corner (see Fig. 4-5). Do not start the second side of the corner at the point. Start along an edge and work toward the point. When turning the point, crease it sharply. I use a hemostat to pinch the fold and make a sharp crease.

After you turn the corner, a flag of seam allowance extends beyond the edge of the appliqué. From the right side of the appliqué cut away the seam allowance flag. It is better to leave a few extra threads than to cut too closely to the appliqué. You can tuck the few extra threads under the point when stitching.

 **Caution**

This method of turning a less-than-90° corner is for machine appliqué only. You can clip a thread or two in the very point of the corner, but then to be secure, those threads require machine stitching.

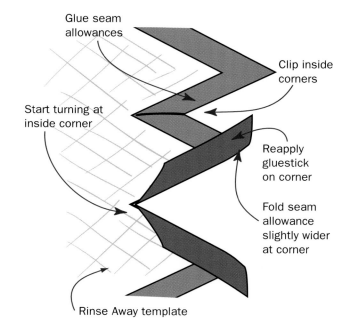

Glue seam allowances

Clip inside corners

Start turning at inside corner

Reapply gluestick on corner

Fold seam allowance slightly wider at corner

Rinse Away template

Fig. 4-6

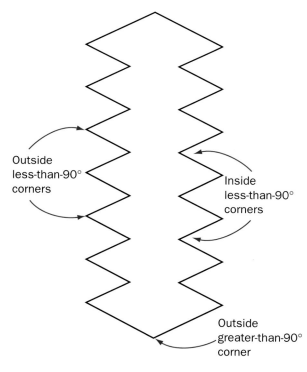

Outside less-than-90° corners

Inside less-than-90° corners

Outside greater-than-90° corner

Fig. 4-5 50% of full size (see Fig. 4-2).

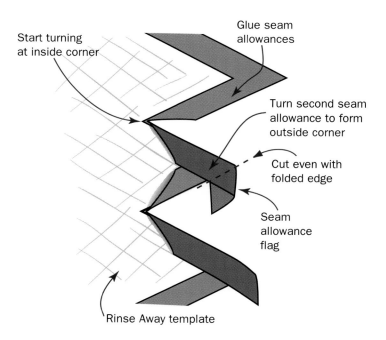

Start turning at inside corner

Glue seam allowances

Turn second seam allowance to form outside corner

Cut even with folded edge

Seam allowance flag

Rinse Away template

Fig. 4-7

INSIDE AND OUTSIDE CURVES

Note that my sample has various sizes of curves (see Fig. 4-8). The large curves are the easiest to do, while the smaller ones are more difficult.

1 Start with the largest curves. On the inside curve *only* make a series of clips. The clips should be at least a thread or two from the edge of the template. Cutting too close to the template weakens the appliqué. Apply gluestick to the wrong side of seam allowances and right side of template edges of the first set of curves.

2 Start with an inside curve. Always start the turns at the crest of the curves, then work the slopes away from the crest. With your finger tips, fold the seam allowance at the bottom of the curve over the template. Make sure the seam allowance "hugs" the inside curve. The seam allowance splits at the clips. Pinch and hold the seam allowance in place until the glue holds. Work halfway up the slope of the curve.

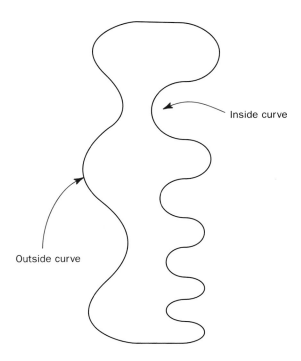

Inside curve

Outside curve

Fig. 4-8 50% of full-size template (see Fig. 4-2).

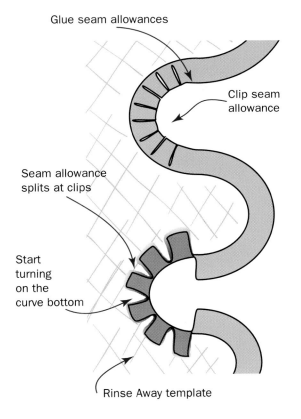

Glue seam allowances

Clip seam allowance

Seam allowance splits at clips

Start turning on the curve bottom

Rinse Away template

Fig. 4-9

3 Skip to the crest or top on the outside curve. With your finger tips, fold the seam allowance at the top of the curve over the template. Pinch and hold the seam allowance in place until the gluestick holds. Work halfway up the slope of the curve. Work up the slope to join the turn from the inside curve.

4 Work across the sample. The smaller outside curves require clipping just like the inside curves. The clips should stop about $\frac{1}{16}$" from the edge of the template. As the curves become smaller the clips need to be closer together. The clipped seam allowances on the outside curves overlap each other, rather than splitting apart like they do on the inside curves. Start at the crest of the curve and turn in the first section of seam allowance. Then turn a section of seam allowance on either side of center. The second and third clipped sections cover the first section. Apply extra glue-stick when necessary.

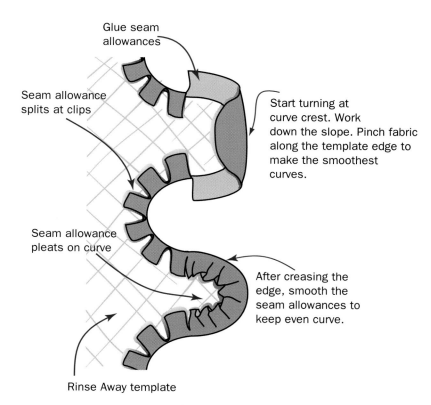

Glue seam allowances

Seam allowance splits at clips

Seam allowance pleats on curve

Start turning at curve crest. Work down the slope. Pinch fabric along the template edge to make the smoothest curves.

After creasing the edge, smooth the seam allowances to keep even curve.

Rinse Away template

Fig. 4-10

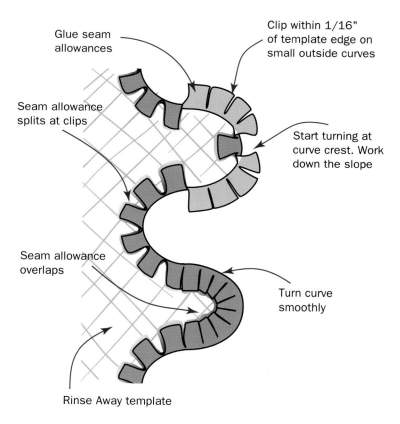

Glue seam allowances

Clip within 1/16" of template edge on small outside curves

Seam allowance splits at clips

Start turning at curve crest. Work down the slope

Seam allowance overlaps

Turn curve smoothly

Rinse Away template

Fig. 4-11

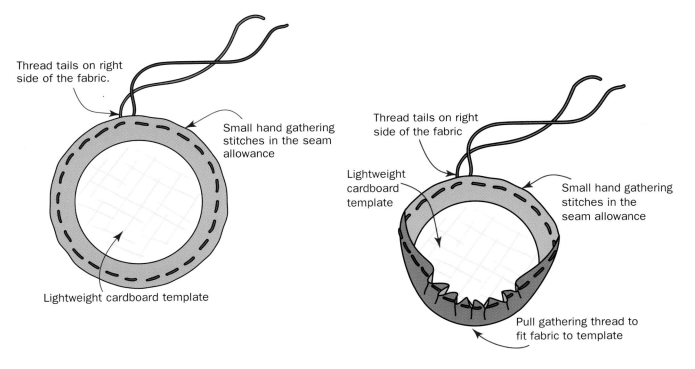

Thread tails on right side of the fabric.

Small hand gathering stitches in the seam allowance

Lightweight cardboard template

Thread tails on right side of the fabric

Lightweight cardboard template

Small hand gathering stitches in the seam allowance

Pull gathering thread to fit fabric to template

Fig. 4-12

Fig. 4-13

TURNING TRUE CIRCLES

This method is the most common method for making true circles. It is also the easiest and most accurate. Rinse Away is too lightweight as the template material for this method. I recommend a lightweight cardboard like a manila folder.

1 Using a circle template as a guide for the true circle, mark the circle on the cardboard and cut out the template.

2 Cut out a fabric circle, adding ¼" seam allowances.

3 By hand, run a gathering thread around the circle in the ¼" seam allowance. Use a running stitch. Smaller stitches result in smoother circles. Leave thread tails at the beginning and end of the stitching.

4 Place the template on the wrong side of the fabric circle and pull the tails of the gathering threads to fit the fabric to the cardboard template. Knot the thread tails together.

5 Press the circle. Use spray starch on the reverse side of the circle to firmly hold the shape. Let the circle cool and dry, then clip and remove the gathering thread.

6 Remove the cardboard template. To keep all appliqué pieces alike, replace the cardboard template with a Rinse Away template prior to stitching the appliqué.

MAKING BIAS TAPE FOR MEDIUM SIZE STEMS

This is a simple no-sew method to making medium-size bias or straight cut strips for stems and baskets. It works well on strips measuring ³/₁₆" or wider. Fold the strips of fabric by pulling them under two pins. The pins work like a rolled hemmer or bias tape turner, and roll in the raw edges. The method requires six long straight pins, a 12" square of heavy muslin, ruler, rotary cutter and mat, hemostat, and a good steam iron.

The secret to this method is using heavy starch when preparing the fabric. The starch facilitates cutting the narrow strips of bias, and it maintains the width of the folded strip.

Note: Like all techniques, this method has lots of little details that make the difference between success and failure. Read all the directions carefully before starting.

1 Heavily starch all fabrics before cutting.

2 Cut the bias or straight strips. To determine the strip width, multiply the finished width by three. Make the cut width generous. I have added an extra ⅛" to the cut strip size:

Finished Size	Cut Size
3/16"	a generous 5/8"
1/4"	7/8"
3/8"	1 1/4"
1/2"	1 5/8"
5/8"	2"
3/4"	2 3/8"

Make each strip as long as possible. Short strips are

extremely difficult to turn evenly. Consider the turned stem strips as yard-age. Don't cut the strip yardage to length until later, when layering the stems for stitching.

3 With the right side out, fold about a 1/2" of the cut strip into thirds lengthwise. The seam allowances overlap. The width of the folded strip should approximately measure the finished size of

the strip. Crease the folds with your fingers or press with the iron.

4 Fold the muslin square in half to make a double layer. On one side of the muslin draw two parallel lines 6" long, equal to the finished width of the strip. Draw these lines with any fine line marker.

5 Place one pin in the muslin on the line end, perpendic-

Bubble Gum Basket block from the *Floral Urns* quilt shows bias tape stems.

ular to the lines. Put the pin into the muslin a short distance from the line. Bring the pin out of the fabric on the first line. Place the folded end of the strip under the pin. The right side of the strip should be against the muslin, the raw edges up. Bring the pin across the strip and into the muslin on the second line. The folded strip fits tightly under the pin.

6 Use the muslin square as a pattern and as protection for the ironing board cover. Pin the muslin to the ironing board to prevent it from moving when pressing the strip. Place the pins on the corners of the muslin.

7 Pull about an inch of the strip under the pin. Finger press the folds in place. Grasp the folded end. Place the point of the iron on the folded strip.

Note: Do not place the iron over the pin. To turn the strip correctly, you must be able to see the pin and where the folds form.

 **Hot Tip**

In this case, a cool tip: To keep from burning your fingers when folding bias strips, grasp the folded edge with a hemostat. The hemostat protects your fingers from the heat and steam of the iron.

8 Hold the unfolded strip, slightly elevated, in your right hand. Place your thumb in the center of the strip about 2" from the pin. Use your fingers to curve the edges of the strip up on either side of your thumb. This gentle curve keeps the strip folding evenly. Holding the iron in place, pull 3" of fabric under the pin.

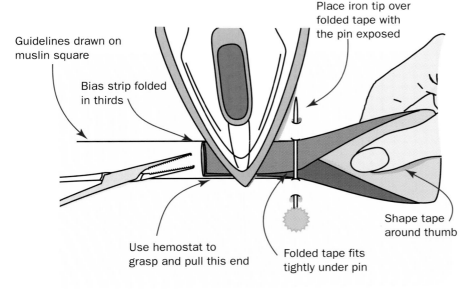

Guidelines drawn on muslin square

Bias strip folded in thirds

Place iron tip over folded tape with the pin exposed

Use hemostat to grasp and pull this end

Folded tape fits tightly under pin

Shape tape around thumb

Fig. 4-14

 **Caution**

Watch out for the steam. Don't place your fingers too close to the iron.

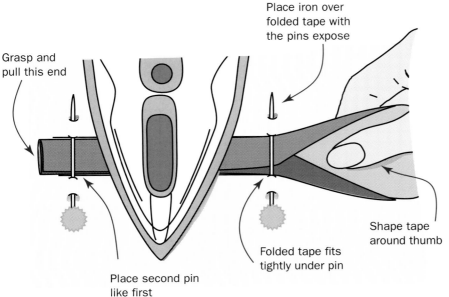

Grasp and pull this end

Place iron over folded tape with the pins expose

Folded tape fits tightly under pin

Shape tape around thumb

Place second pin like first

Fig. 4-15

9 Remove the iron. Place a second pin like the first, about 3" away from the first pin. Place the folded end of the strip under the second pin.

10 Hold the iron in the space between the pins and continue pulling the strip to fold.

 ## Caution

The iron is resting on the ironing board. It can cause scorching. I recommend using a large muslin press cloth over the ironing board to protect the ironing board cover.

 ## Hot Tip

To make tapes faster, I recommend the Clover Bias Tape Makers. They come in five widths: 2", 1", ¾", ½", and ¼". Starch the fabric before cutting. The starch makes the tape easier to fold and ensures that the tape is crisp and even.

MAKING A FINISHED END FOR BIAS TAPE STEMS

Occasionally, a stem requires a finished end. For stems made from folded bias tape, make the turned bias tape. Using the pattern, determine the length of stem required and add a minimum of 1" to that measure. Cut the stem to length.

Unfold the turned stem. On one short end of the stem turn and press a ¼" seam allowance to the wrong side of the fabric. This makes the finished end. Refold the turned stem and press.

MAKING PIPING FOR TINY STEMS

This is my all-time favorite way to make tiny stems. I was inspired by the Superfine Stems method in Elly Sienkiewicz's book *Baltimore Beauties and Beyond.* I combined her technique with an old mini-piping technique and realized I could make perfect small stems as fast as I could machine stitch. The stems are made with corded piping. After making the piping and stitching it in place, remove the cord, leaving a perfectly uniform stem. The technique is suitable for stems that are ¹/₁₆" to ¹/₈" wide and is applicable for stems up to ¼" wide. The method requires a grooved presser foot, cording, rotary cutter, ruler, and mat.

There are many variables to this method. The basic directions are the principles of making mini piping. For specifics on feet and machine directions, see page 11.

1 For all mini piping cut a strip of lightly starched stem fabric at least 1" wide. For wider stems cut the strip 1" wider than the finished width of the stem. Make each strip as long as possible; short strips are difficult to turn evenly. Consider the strips as yardage. Don't cut the strip yardage to length until later, when layering the stems for stitching.

2 Make the piping by folding the strip of fabric over a cord. The secret to good piping is stitching the fabric firmly around the cord without stitching into the cord. To help achieve this effect, guide the cord into a groove on the bottom of any presser foot with a groove, or use a zipper foot. The foot holds the fabric taut to the cord and prevents the cord from slipping under the needle and being caught in the stitching line.

3 Fold the stem fabric, right side out, around the cord. For

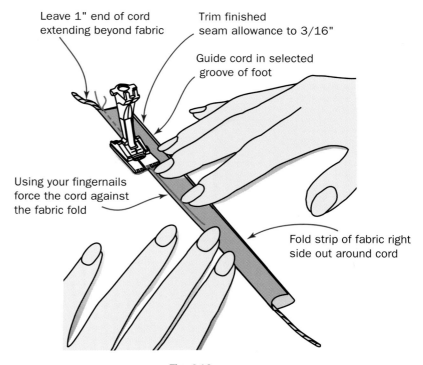

Leave 1" end of cord extending beyond fabric

Trim finished seam allowance to 3/16"

Guide cord in selected groove of foot

Using your fingernails force the cord against the fabric fold

Fold strip of fabric right side out around cord

Fig. 4-16

my example I used size 3 perle cotton. The cord should extend 1" beyond the edge of the fabric. Slip the cord and fabric under the presser foot. (See Fig. 4-16.)

4 Place the cord in the selected groove of the foot. Hold the seam allowances toward the right. Using a straight stitch, sew along the cord, making the piping.

USING THE PINTUCK FOOT

My favorite way to make mini piping is to use a pintuck foot. For these directions I'm using a seven-groove pintuck foot. Pintuck feet, including three-groove, five-groove, seven-groove, and nine-groove feet, make the best mini piping. The grooves are deep and the foot sits firmly on the feed dogs. With the machine correctly set up, it is almost impossible to stitch into the cord when using these feet. Pintuck feet have centered grooves. With the cord in the center groove and the needle in center position, the needle will stitch into the cord. The key to successfully using this foot is to adjust the needle position to stitch directly beside the cord, not through it. These feet work best with variable needle positions, especially those machines with seven or more needle positions.

To know how much to adjust the needle, place a length of cord, without fabric, under the center groove. Now adjust the needle position to the right until it just clears the cord. The cord should fit easily into the groove without too much extra space. The cord should not bind in the groove but freely move forward and backward. This will be a different setting for each size of pintuck foot. Try placing the cord in any groove other than center.

Machine Savvy

HELP! MY MACHINE DOESN'T HAVE VARIABLE NEEDLE POSITIONS.

It is possible to fool the machine into adjusting the needle position. Use the double needle recommended for the size of the pintuck foot. (The foot directions recommend the needle size.) Thread only the right needle; ignore the left needle. Threading only the right needle fools the machine into a right hand needle position. Stitch the piping as if there were only a single needle in the machine, following the basic directions for making mini piping. If the stitch tension is not perfect, try reversing the cord and fabric, threading only the left needle, and try stitching on the opposite side of the cord.

The double needle sizes for the most common pintuck feet are 2.0/80 or 2.5/80 for the 5 groove foot, and 1.6/70 or 2.0/80 for the 7 groove foot.

Hot Tip

I never throw away double needles when I have broken only one of the needles. Even broken, they have uses!

Machine Savvy

WHAT DO THE NUMBERS ON THE SIZES OF A DOUBLE NEEDLE MEAN?

The number before the slash is the distance between the needles. It is in millimeters like the zigzag width. The second number, after the slash, is the size of each of the needles.

PIPING HINTS

There are a few things that make it simpler to stitch the piping. As a novice at the technique, consider the beginning and end of the piping as waste. The cord and fabric don't feed evenly unless they are under the complete length of the presser foot. Usually the cord catches in the beginning stitching of the piping.

To have the fabric firmly stitched around the cord, before sewing, smooth the cord against the center fold of the fabric by rubbing the piping between the thumb and index finger of your left hand. After smoothing the piping with your left hand, lay the piping against the bed of the machine. Force the cord against the fold of the fabric, using the fingernails of your right hand. Hold the piping firmly against the bed of the machine directly in front of the presser foot.

Upon completion of the piping, remove the piping from the machine. Do not pull out the cord filler. Trim the seam allowance to $^1/_4$".

STITCHING THE PIPING TO THE BLOCK

Position the completed piping in the correct location on the background fabric. *Do not* cut the

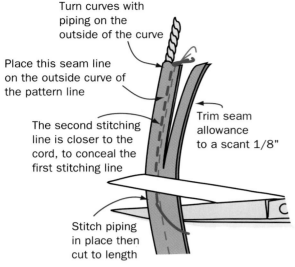

Turn curves with piping on the outside of the curve

Place this seam line on the outside curve of the pattern line

The second stitching line is closer to the cord, to conceal the first stitching line

Trim seam allowance to a scant 1/8"

Stitch piping in place then cut to length

Fig. 4-17

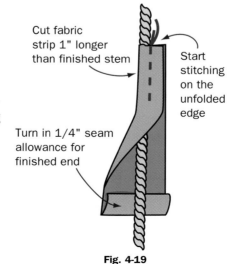

Tip folded edge over the seam allowances. Press in place. Appliqué along the folded edge.

Remove the cord

Fig. 4-18

piping strip to length; work with the yardage. *Do not* remove the cord filler. Line up the stitching line of the piping along one edge of the stem. For the best curved stems, stitch with the piping to the outside curve, and the seam allowance to the inside curve.

Using the same foot used to make the piping, stitch the piping to the background. Cut the piping to length and remove the cord. Trim the excess seam allowance to a scant $1/8$" and tip the folded edge over the seam allowance. Hand or machine appliqué the folded edge in place.

Advanced Methods: Occasionally, the first line of stitching used to make the piping can be seen when tipping the piping over to complete the appliqué. Correct this by using multiple needle positions. When making the piping, use a needle position that is one setting farther to the right than the finished piping. Then move the needle position to the correct position when stitching the piping to the background fabric. This conceals the first line of stitching in the seam allowances and ensures a firm even piping for the stem.

MAKING A FINISHED END FOR PIPING STEMS

Frequently, stems begin and end under other appliqué pieces. Occasionally, a stem requires a finished end. Unlike other piped stems, a finished end requires piping made to length. Make the piping strips specifically for each stem.

Determine the length of piping required. Add a minimum of 1" to that measure. Cut and prepare the piping fabric according to the basic instructions (see page 36). On one short end of the piping fabric turn and press a $1/4$" seam allowance to

Cut fabric strip 1" longer than finished stem

Start stitching on the unfolded edge

Turn in 1/4" seam allowance for finished end

Fig. 4-19

the wrong side of the fabric. This makes the finished end.

Start stitching the piping on the unfinished end of the piping and stitch toward the finished end. This gives the neatest end. Stitch carefully when approaching the finished end and use four or five reverse stitches to secure the end.

When stitching the stem in place on the block, begin stitching on the finished end to ensure the correct placement. For the least conspicuous start and knot, begin stitching at least $1/8$" from the finished end. Make the first few stitches in reverse, stitching toward the exact finished end of the stem, then stitch forward to complete the stem.

MAKING LOOPS IN PIPING STEMS

Many fine stems, like grape tendrils, have loops. The cord in the piping causes problems when looped. To simply follow the basic directions would result in permanently stitching the cord into the stem, making finishing the stem impossible. To make a successful loop, partially remove the cord and fold the stem during stitching.

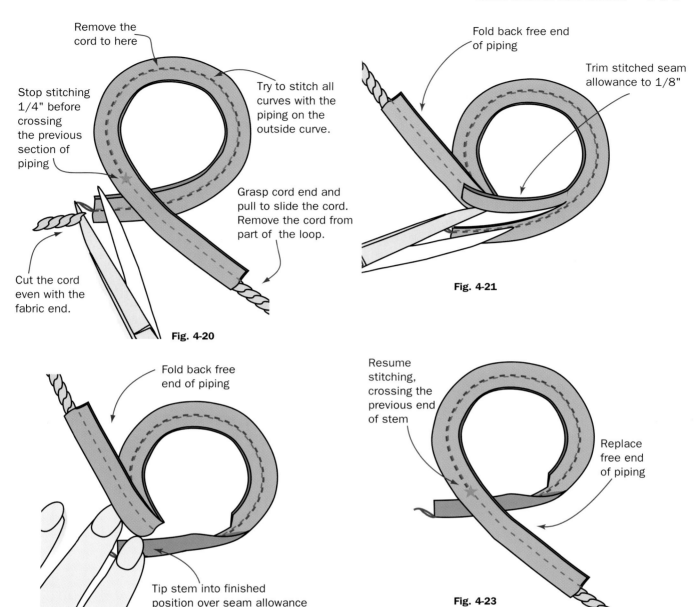

Remove the cord to here

Stop stitching 1/4" before crossing the previous section of piping

Try to stitch all curves with the piping on the outside curve.

Cut the cord even with the fabric end.

Grasp cord end and pull to slide the cord. Remove the cord from part of the loop.

Fig. 4-20

Fold back free end of piping

Trim stitched seam allowance to 1/8"

Fig. 4-21

Fold back free end of piping

Tip stem into finished position over seam allowance

Fig. 4-22

Resume stitching, crossing the previous end of stem

Replace free end of piping

Fig. 4-23

1 Stitch the stem in place on the block background to within ¼" before the spot where the stem crosses a previously stitched section of piping. Stop stitching with the needle lowered in the fabric.

2 To reduce the amount of cord that you have to pull through, clip any cord that may extend beyond the beginning end of the piping. Gently pull on the other end of the cord to slide it out of the stitched piping.

Do not remove the cord from the unstitched sections of piping. Be careful not to remove the cord beyond the last stitch or the needle. The cord should move without having to raise the foot.

 Hot Tip

Bernina and New Home 9000 owners can use the knee lifter to partially raise the presser foot and keep both hands free to adjust the cord.

3 Using small sharp scissors, clip away the excess seam allowance on the stitched section of the piping stem.

4 With your fingers, tip the stem over the seam allowance into its finished position.

5 Continue stitching the piping to the background, stitching across the previously stitched section.

39

Caution

Working at the machine with the needle in the work may be difficult for the inexperienced stitcher. You can raise the foot if the cord is not sliding freely. If you're having problems working at the machine, you can cut threads and completely remove the fabrics from the machine.

PRESSER FOOT OPTIONS FOR PIPING STEMS

The thickness of the cord determines the size of the piping. However, cord size also affects what foot you use. The groove size in the foot should be equal to the cord size. The cord should fit easily into the groove without too much extra space. The cord should not bind in the groove but freely move forward and backward. Approach the cord and foot relationship two ways. Choose a cord size to match the groove in the foot, or choose a foot to match the cord size.

Choosing a cord. Any smooth cord will work as a filler for piping. The cord does not remain in the piping so it can be any color and does not have to be washable.

I recommend perle cotton size 3 or 5, buttonhole twist, Cordonnet, crochet cottons, store string, packaging cord, cable cord, or macramé cord. (I have used even fine wire as a filler.) I don't recommend fuzzy low twist fillers like knitting yarn.

When the cord is too thin in relationship to the foot, the piping is flat and the fabric not tightly wrapped around the cord. When the cord is too thick for the foot, the foot does not feed the fabric forward and the needle stitches through the cord.

Choosing a foot. The following is a list of grooved feet and basic directions on how to use these feet:

Appliqué foot: This foot has a narrow centered groove like a pintuck foot. Follow the pintuck foot instructions to use this foot (see page 37).

Invisible zipper foot or basic buttonhole foot: Both these feet have grooves that are to the left or right of center. Follow the basic directions for using center needle position.

Piping foot or welting foot: These feet make medium to large piping, usually over $1/4$" in diameter. There are many foot designs called piping or welting feet. It is impossible to give specific directions for all the variations, although the basic use of the foot is always the same.

Look at the groove in the foot to determine if the foot has a centered groove or a right/left groove. All center groove feet require variable needle positions. Choose a cord to fit the foot. Follow the foot directions that came with the foot and your machine. Make and stitch the piping to the block background using the general directions.

Beading foot: The beading foot attaches strands or strings of beads. It has a centered groove like the appliqué foot. This foot is available in different sizes depending on the intended use and requires variable needle positions.

Basic zipper foot: This is the foot of last resort when making mini piping. It does work reasonably well for the larger piping. With practice the piping may be even, but the fabric is not firmly wrapped around the cord. Attach the foot or move the needle position so the sole of the foot is to the right of the needle. Guide the cord to the left of the foot, with the seam allowances under the foot. Follow the general piping directions for using the piping.

CHAPTER 5
Raw-Edge Appliqué

RAW-EDGE APPLIQUÉ is the perfect choice for machine appliqué. Machine stitching can securely hold the cut edge. It doesn't require a turned edge for strength or aesthetics. It has a definite advantage over turned-edge appliqué: The appliqué finishes exactly as it is cut. Without seam allowances, the shape of the appliqué pieces is sharp and well defined. Compared to turned seam allowances that can distort the pieces by softening the curves and points, the cut edges are super accurate for the most difficult corners, points and tiny pieces. The technique can produce effects and designs that would be difficult or impossible with turned-edge methods. This chapter explains how to prepare raw-edge appliqué pieces. For stitching techniques turn to Chapter 6.

I have done raw-edge appliqué for over 25 years, long before I took up hand appliqué. I love its speed and accuracy. It is the method of appliqué I used on my quilt, *Floral Urns*. This quilt won the Bernina Award for the Best Machine Workmanship at the 1993 American Quilter's Society Show.

The method is wonderful, but it is not identical to turned edge appliqué. The lack of turned edges makes the technique accurate, but it also affects the appearance of the finished appliqué. The design is less dimensional because it lacks the slight raise imparted by the seam allowances. The well

defined and flatter edges can make the appliqué appear printed or painted rather than stitched. Some quilters tell me they dislike the crisp, clean look of raw-edge appliqué. It lacks the soft, raised effect they have come to equate with appliqué. Other quilters express an opposite view and love the neat, accurate results. Whatever your opinion, raw-edge appliqué has its advantages and is extremely well suited to detailed patterns and broderie perse.

Sew A Sample

RAW-EDGE APPLIQUÉ SAMPLE

Supplies

- Cotton fabrics, lightly starched and pressed for the appliqué

- Prepared block background and pattern from basic appliqué instructions on page 20

- Pigma 01 pen, mechanical pencil, or other fine line marker

- Gluestick

- Circle template

- Teflon pressing sheet

- Paper-backed fusible web

You can use any paper backed fusible web, but not all webbing gives good results. I prefer HTC Fusible Web for all my own appliqués. HTC Fusible Web is securely bonded to the paper backing and tightly adheres the fabric layers.

Hot Tip

Fusible webs are not created equal. To ensure the best results, choose a fusible that is securely adhered to the paper backing. Test your fusible to make sure small appliqué pieces stay adhered throughout the handling and repeated heating that occurs during layering and pressing complex designs.

BASICS OF PREPARATION FOR RAW-EDGE METHOD OF APPLIQUÉ

Since fusible web became popular in the 1960s, it has drastically changed the way we do machine appliqué. Fusible web securely bonds the appliqué fabric to the background. The stitching no longer plays a primary role in appliqué. Its main purpose is to supplement the fusible web by preventing the fused edges from peeling or raveling. As a result, the appliqué stitch has evolved from a wide, conspicuous satin stitch, to a discreet, almost invisible, zigzag or buttonhole stitch.

Initially, the use of fusible web appliqué brought a host of problems to quiltmaking. Extensive use of fusible web makes the appliqué less pliable. The effect is acceptable on simple designs, but multi-layered designs like Baltimore Album blocks become too stiff to quilt. The appliqué and finished quilts often lack the soft hand and characteristic drape of hand done quilts. There is a simple solution to all these problems. This method combines the best of fusible web, with the look and feel of hand appliqué.

I exclusively use a fusible web method called *outlining*. It is based on the premise that fusible web, like hand stitching, is only needed on the edges of the appliqué. The appliqués are securely fused to the background with a narrow outline or "doughnut" of fusible web. The centers of the appliqué pieces are left unattached. The appliqués are secure yet pliable. The method is extremely simple, efficient, and conserves fusible web.

In the example (see Fig. 5-1), a twelve petal flower illustrates the basic directions on how to make a fusible web "doughnut." In its simplest form the doughnut has a shallow 1/4" seam allowance on both the interior and exterior of the finished edge of the appliqué. The interior seam allowance holds the appliqué. The exterior seam allowance is used during the fusing and cutting steps. The exterior seam allowance adds strength and stability to the fusible web doughnut and makes it easier to handle.

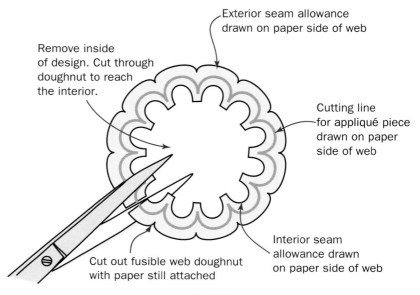

Remove inside of design. Cut through doughnut to reach the interior.

Exterior seam allowance drawn on paper side of web

Cutting line for appliqué piece drawn on paper side of web

Interior seam allowance drawn on paper side of web

Cut out fusible web doughnut with paper still attached

Fig. 5-1

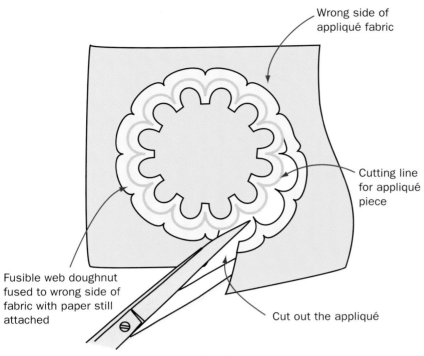

Wrong side of
appliqué fabric

Cutting line
for appliqué
piece

Fusible web doughnut
fused to wrong side of
fabric with paper still
attached

Cut out the appliqué

Fig. 5-2

BASIC OUTLINING METHOD

Always store your fusibles in a roll, loosely secured with a rubber band, rather than folded. If the fusible web should separate from the backing paper, it can be re-adhered by pressing using a Teflon sheet. Place the fusible, paper side up, on the pressing sheet. Press lightly using an iron on the cotton setting. Let the paper, web, and Teflon sheet completely cool. Then carefully peel the web and paper off the pressing sheet.

The directions for the basic outlining method are as follows:

1 To trace the individual pieces to the fusible web, write on the paper side of the web, using a fine line pencil or Pigma pen. Trace the pieces from the *reverse* side of the pattern. I suggest using a distinct dotted line to mark the edges overlapped by other pieces in the appliqué

because the exterior seam allowances on these edges will fall under other pieces. Mark every fusible web piece with its pattern number.

2 Add a ¼" seam allowance to the exterior of all the pieces. Every piece has two lines: a line indicating the exact shape of the appliqué piece, and a line indicating the ¼" exterior seam allowance.

3 Overlapped edges require special handling to reduce the fusible web to a minimum. When cutting the external seam allowance, do not add the seam allowance to overlapped edges. The overlapped edges have only the interior seam allowance. Mark as a distinct dotted line so these edges are easy to locate. Cut on the dotted line. This reduces the fusible web in the overlapped sections. The simple bud pattern in Fig. 5-3 illustrates how to cut an overlapped edge.

Advanced Method: The exterior seam allowance makes the fusible web doughnut easier to handle. It is cut away in the following steps, so it isn't necessary to be super accurate in the amount of web left around the outside edge. To cut down on the amount of drawing, simply "eye" the ¹/₄" seam allowance when cutting out

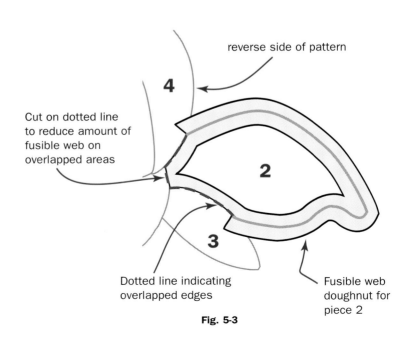

reverse side of pattern

Cut on dotted line
to reduce amount of
fusible web on
overlapped areas

Dotted line indicating
overlapped edges

Fusible web
doughnut for
piece 2

Fig. 5-3

the piece. Just don't forget to allow for the exterior seam allowance when drawing other pieces or cutting out the piece!

4 Cut out the fusible web pieces on the exterior seam allowance line.

5 This step is cutting the "hole" in the doughnut:

Remove the fusible web on the interior of the appliqué by cutting a slim $\frac{1}{4}$" seam allowance along the interior of the appliqué. There should be a $\frac{1}{4}$" seam allowance on each side of the finished design line (see Fig. 5-3).

Sewing Savvy

When cutting out the interior fusible web, simply cut through the doughnut to reach the interior of the design. Don't try to punch through fusible web or fold the fusible web to cut out the center. These methods peel the fusible off the paper.

6 Press the fusible web doughnut to the wrong side of the appliqué fabric. Follow the manufacturer's directions for a secure bond.

7 Cut out the appliqué on the finished design line, except for the *overlapped edges* marked with the dotted line. On these edges add an $\frac{1}{4}$" seam allowance. This allows for extra fabric to form the overlap.

8 Remove the paper backing from the appliqué. Position the appliqué piece in the correct location and press in place following the manufacturer's instructions.

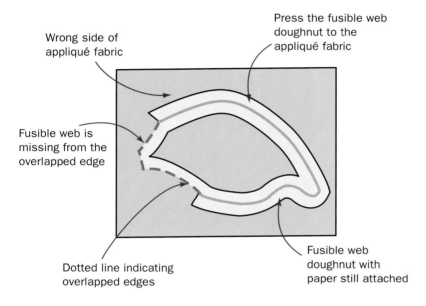

Wrong side of appliqué fabric

Press the fusible web doughnut to the appliqué fabric

Fusible web is missing from the overlapped edge

Dotted line indicating overlapped edges

Fusible web doughnut with paper still attached

Fig. 5-4

TRUE CIRCLES IN RAW-EDGE APPLIQUÉ

Draw the circle with a circle template. Follow the basic instructions for making the fusible doughnut. As the circles become smaller it is more difficult to cut out the centers. With circles under $\frac{1}{2}$", I use a new sharp paper punch to punch out the hole rather than cutting it out with scissors. Paper punches are available in a number of sizes and are great for removing the centers of any tiny pieces.

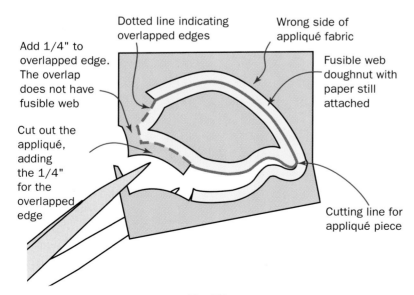

Add 1/4" to overlapped edge. The overlap does not have fusible web

Dotted line indicating overlapped edges

Wrong side of appliqué fabric

Fusible web doughnut with paper still attached

Cut out the appliqué, adding the 1/4" for the overlapped edge

Cutting line for appliqué piece

Fig. 5-5

STEMS IN RAW-EDGE APPLIQUÉ

Fine stems pose a problem in raw-edge appliqué. It is impossible to use a doughnut of fusible on a piece that is only ½" wide. There is really only one workable alternative. Forget outlining and use

fusible web behind the entire stem. It's fast and neat, but does make the stem very flat. An occasional flat stem is unnoticeable, but you might choose the folded edge method for designs with "miles" of stems or strip baskets.

Advanced Methods: If you're like me, you want to do those wonderful woven strip baskets found on Baltimore Album quilts.

These baskets are a nightmare to make with strips of raw-edge pieces. Unlike folded strips, fused strips do not easily curve or shape. In addition, weaving results in multiple layers of fusible web pieces. The woven section of the basket gets very unyielding.

There is a better way to do this. Cut the woven section of the basket from one fabric piece. To

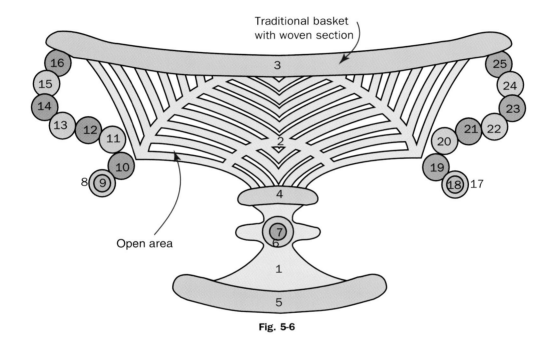

Fig. 5-6

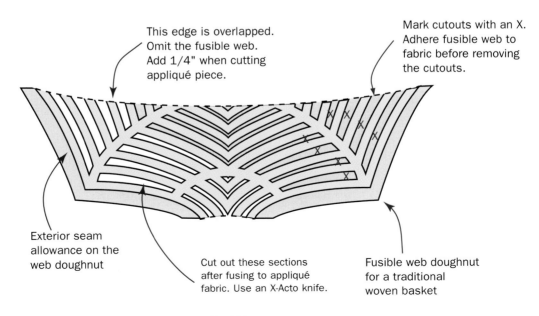

Fig. 5-7

make the spaces between the strips, cut holes in the fabric. Although it requires a steady hand and a cool head to cut neat and accurate holes in the center of a fabric piece, this method solves most problems. The basket maintains its shape because it is a single piece of fabric. Also the basket is as soft as possible because it uses a single layer of fabric and fusible web. The best way to approach this technique is by fusing the entire basket section to the appliqué fabric, then removing the small sections of fabric and fusible from between the strips.

Occasionally I see a basket that has a strip or two in a second color, rather than all the strips in a single color. With careful planning, it is possible to do two colored baskets by cutting away the second colored sections from the first basket and replacing or weaving them with the second color strips before pressing the basket in place.

 ## Hot Tip

I use an "X" to mark the hole spaces on the fusible web. I use an X-Acto knife to cut the holes. Place the basket, wrong side up, on a rotary cutting mat and use a *new* blade in the knife. Press firmly and move slowly. After cutting out the holes, remove the paper backing and fuse the basket in place.

BRODERIE PERSE

Historically, broderie perse appliqué used printed motifs like flowers and leaves cut from expensive chintz fabrics. Designs were made by appliquéing the printed motifs on a plain fabric

background. The appliqué was combined with plain fabric appliqué and pieced borders or blocks. This method gave the quilter a sense of creativity and extended the use of expensive fabrics. The most distinctive feature of antique broderie perse quilts is that the raw-edge pieces are appliquéd with a tiny buttonhole stitch.

 ## Sew A Sample

BRODERIE PERSE SAMPLE

Supplies

- Print fabric such as chintz, home decorating fabrics

- Cotton square for background

- Fusible web

- Light box

- Fine scissors

- Pins

- Gluestick

Broderie perse is perfect for a raw-edge method like fusible outlining. Contemporary quilters still use chintz fabrics for broderie perse. An excellent source for appliqués is upholstery and drapery fabrics. The large scale and exquisite colors and prints work extremely well. The fabric should be a firmly woven cotton or cotton blend. To prepare the motifs for appliqué requires a light box.

1 Cut out the chosen motif adding at least ¼" around the

Broderie perse in progress. The printed fabric is placed right side down on a light box. The design is clearly visible to be traced to the paper-backed fusible web.

outside edges of the motif.

2 Place the motif right side down on the light box or light table. Place the fusible web, paper side up, on the motif. (Note, the fusible web is *not* ironed on.) On the paper, using a pencil, trace around the outside edge of the motif. Move the paper off the motif and cut out the paper doughnut. You are substituting the fabric print for a design, instead of using a drawn pattern.

Advanced Methods: When two fabric print motifs touch, you can use both of them. Cut and trace the two motifs as one unit. Mark the finished edge the two motifs share and allow a $1/4$" interior seam allowance on both sides of the marked line. In the simplest form the fusible looks much like the number 8.

4 Using the light box, correctly place the fusible over the printed motif. Use pins or a dot of gluestick to hold the fusible in place while moving the appliqué to the ironing board.

5 Press the fusible web doughnut to the wrong side of the appliqué fabric. Follow the manufacturer's directions for a secure bond.

6 Cut out the appliqué on the finished design line. Remove the paper and press the appliqué in place on the quilt top.

Finished broderie perse.

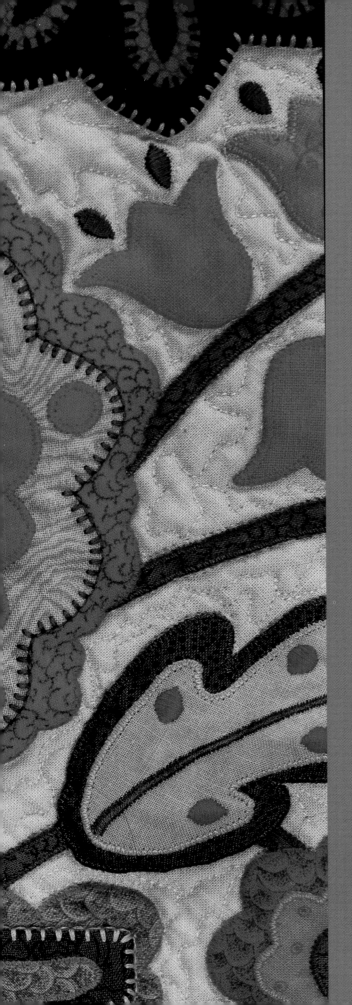

Part Three

Appliqué Stitches & Stitching

CHAPTER 6

Invisible Stitches for Appliqué

THIS CHAPTER PRESENTS in depth directions on invisibly stitching the appliqué to the background fabric. The stitches work equally well for turned-edge or raw-edge appliqué.

 Sew A Sample

INVISIBLY STITCHING THE APPLIQUÉ SAMPLE

Supplies

- Open toe embroidery foot

- Invisible thread or fine machine embroidery thread

- Fine machine embroidery thread to match the background fabric

- One 18" square of cotton fabric to use as background

- Freezer paper

- Gluestick

- Use the appliqué samples made in previous Sew A Sample sections

Machine Setup

Narrow, short zigzag stitch

Stitch width 1.5

Stitch length 1.0

Center needle position

Open toe or no-bridge embroidery foot

A number of machine stitches can be used to hold the appliqué in place. Blindhem and overlock are frequent choices. Personally, I prefer simple zigzag.

 Sewing Savvy

WHY I DON'T USE BLINDHEM AND OVERLOCK STITCHES FOR APPLIQUÉ.

Both of these stitches have a short section of straight stitching divided by a zigzag (see Fig. 6-1). The straight stitches cause the problems in appliqué. The straight stitches form a small gap between the zigzag stitches. The gap does reduce the number of times the needle pierces the fabric, and that helps the appliqué look more like its handmade counterpart. The straight stitches are great on long straight edges, but they can cause problems on corners and tiny pieces. It is difficult to judge where the zigzag stitches are going to fall on the appliqué. For the strongest appliqué, the zigzags should be at the inner and outer points of the corners. Frequently, what actually happens is that the straight stitches fall at the very point of the corner. This means the corners are not secure.

The stitch length also causes problems in the straight stitch sections. By design, the blindhem and overlock stitches have at least a $1/4$" gap between the zigzag stitches. That size gap is too large for small appliqué pieces. When you reduce the stitch length to correct the

spacing, the straight stitches become very tiny. These small straight stitches pull the bobbin thread up to the top of the fabric. With invisible thread in the needle the problem can be even more pronounced. The results are a dotted line of bobbin thread running along all the edges of the appliqué. It gives the appearance of poor thread tension.

FAVORITE METHOD FOR INVISIBLE STITCHING

The simple zigzag stitch has a number of advantages over other stitches. It corners well and has easy tension adjustments. The following is my favorite method to invisibly stitch the appliqué:

1 Thread the machine with a bobbin thread that matches the background. Thread the needle with invisible thread or thread to match the appliqué.

 Hot Tip

With the proper tension adjustment, you can always use background colored thread in the bobbin. This saves on the number of bobbins needed for a project, and the time it takes to exchange bobbins for every color change of needle thread.

2 Set up the machine for a narrow short zigzag. The basic metric settings are 1.5 width and 1.0 length, with a center needle position.

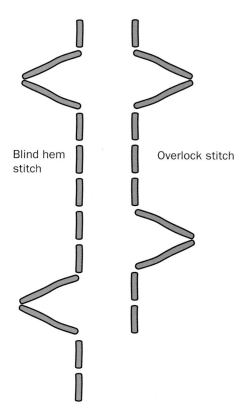

Blind hem stitch   Overlock stitch

Fig. 6-1

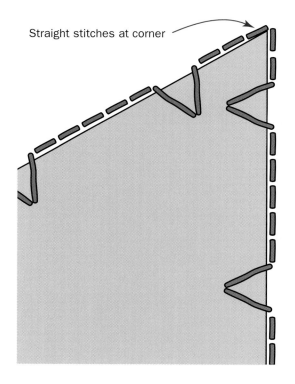

Straight stitches at corner

Fig. 6-2

Detail of sample made to practice invisible stitching techniques.

Advanced Methods: The stitch size depends on your skill and the look you're trying to achieve. A narrower stitch width and shorter stitch length give less conspicuous results. With increased skill you can reduce the width and length. The smallest stitch I recommend for turned edge appliqué is .75 width with .5 length. The smallest stitch I recommend for raw edge appliqué is 1.0 width with .5 length. I use a 1.0 width with .75 length for almost all my appliqué. The stitch is fine enough to be almost invisible, yet wide enough to be secure and easy to guide.

3 Use the open toe or no-bridge embroidery foot on the machine. When making the sample, use the 18" square of cotton fabric as background for the three appliqué pieces prepared in the folded-edge method of the previous sections. Press the freezer paper to the wrong side of the background. Using glue-stick, glue the turned edge appliqués to the background fabric. You can substitute raw edge appliqués for the turned edge appliqués.

4 Stitch through the center of a sample appliqué piece. Sew a 3" line of zigzag at your preferred setting. Remove the sample from the machine and check the thread tensions.

 **Hot Tip**

To correctly adjust the tension, sew a sample in fabric identical to the appliqué, including the backing and template materials. It is so tempting to cheat and simply sew a line of stitching on any scrap piece of plain fabric. My advice: don't cheat!

5 Adjust the thread tension for perfect stitching.

HINTS FOR ADJUSTING THREAD TENSION

Loosen the top thread tension so the top thread pulls slightly to the wrong side of the fabric.

Loosening the tension has three positive effects:

❑ It allows the use of a basic color bobbin thread. The bobbin thread stays on the wrong side of the appliqué.

❑ It gives a smooth, even stitch by pulling the stitch knot to the wrong side of the fabric.

❑ It relaxes the tension on the stitches. This gives a softer edge to the appliqué and is less apt to pucker or distort the finished block.

To determine the correct thread tensions, first look at the sample stitching. The bobbin thread should not be visible on the right side of the appliqué. Next, look at the wrong side of stitching. Mentally, divide the zigzag width into thirds. On each side of the stitch, the top thread should be one third the width of the zigzag. The bobbin thread should be in the center third of the stitch, but should not be a straight line.

Some machines have special tension adjustments marked for making buttonholes. These pre-marked adjustments can be a great starting place for the appliqué tension. In other machines, the upper tension dial has a section marked for making buttonholes. This loosened needle tension is frequently the correct setting for the appliqué stitch.

In some machines you can thread a small hole on a finger of the bobbin case when making buttonholes. Thread this hole to adjust the tensions, although this tightens the bobbin tension rather than loosening the needle tension. I frequently combine this feature with loosened thread tension.

❑ Before turning the tension dial, write down the current setting. This marks the normal setting and ensures the successful return to basic sewing.

❑ Turn the tension down by small increments. Turn no more than a whole number at a time.

Machine Savvy

HOW DO I ADJUST THE TOP THREAD TENSION?

Most machines have a numbered upper tension dial. The lower the number, the looser the tension. If your machine does not have a numbered dial, there is a saying that can help you remember which way to turn the dial for the effect. "Righty Tighty, Lefty Loosey." (OK, it is not Shakespeare, but it works!)

Sew A Sample

TENSION ADJUSTMENTS SAMPLE

Supplies

• 6" x 3" piece of light-colored cotton broadcloth

• 1 piece of typing paper

Machine setup

Thread the machine with contrasting thread in the bobbin and in the needle. Mismatched thread makes it easier to see the individual stitches.

It is easiest to do tension adjustments in a continuous line, like the stitch length sample on page 4. Draw six lines 1" apart on the background fabric. Sew each section at a different tension setting. Write down the setting used for that section. When you have finished stitching a line, check the sample.

You should make this sample before sewing any project, to help you choose

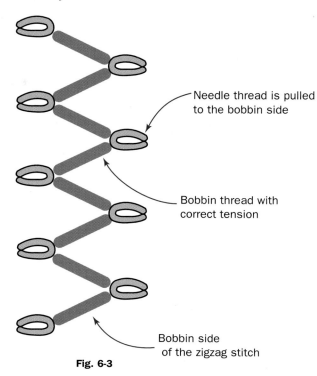

Needle thread is pulled to the bobbin side

Bobbin thread with correct tension

Bobbin side of the zigzag stitch

Fig. 6-3

the correct tension setting. Remember that your sample fabric and any backing must match that of your project. If none of the tension samples seem correct, continue adjusting the tensions as you sew another line of stitching.

STITCHING THE APPLIQUÉ

There are three key areas to successfully stitching the appliqué: 1. Securing the threads at the beginning and end of a line of stitching, 2. Placing stitches on the appliqué piece, and 3. Properly turning corners and curves.

Securing threads. To secure the threads at the beginning and end of a line of stitching, turn the stitch width to zero to make a straight stitch at the same stitch length as for the zigzag stitch. Make six to eight straight stitches in the background *only*. Place the straight stitches as close as possible to the appliqué piece. For turned-edge appliqué, try to begin and end the stitching under another piece.

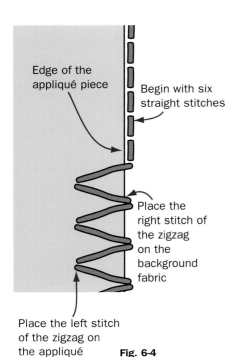

Edge of the appliqué piece

Begin with six straight stitches

Place the right stitch of the zigzag on the background fabric

Place the left stitch of the zigzag on the appliqué

Fig. 6-4

When joining a previous stitching line, zigzag a few stitches over the previous stitches and then change to straight stitch and sew three or four stitches over the previous zigzag.

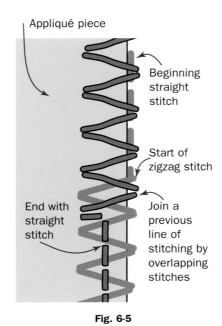

Appliqué piece

Beginning straight stitch

Start of zigzag stitch

Join a previous line of stitching by overlapping stitches

End with straight stitch

Fig. 6-5

Stitch placement. The stitch placement on the appliqué piece should be one stitch on the appliqué, one stitch off the appliqué. When stitching clockwise around the appliqué, the needle in the right hand swing should pierce *only* the background fabric, yet be as close as possible to the appliqué edge.

Note: To make the directions uniform, all the illustrations and directions are for clockwise stitching.

 Sewing Savvy

Appliqué is a right hand or left hand skill. Most people stitch clockwise around the appliqué pieces. There isn't really a rule about the stitching direction. The appliqué

can be stitched equally well counterclockwise, although I suspect the clockwise turns are natural and easier for right handed people. By design, the sewing machine is for right handed people and right handed stitching. Just think about it. The dials are on the right, the hand wheel is on the right, and the larger sewing surface is on the left.

Properly turn corners and curves. To properly turn corners and curves, consider that there are four kinds of corners and two curves. The bite or stitch width for this stitching is very narrow. It is important to correctly stitch the curves and corners to give the maximum amount of strength to the stitching.

Sew A Sample

APPLIQUÉ CORNERS AND CURVES SAMPLE

Appliqué the samples prepared in previous sections, using the following directions for corners and curves.

INSIDE AND OUTSIDE CURVES

Successful curves require the stitches to be perpendicular to the edge of the appliqué. Place the stitches like cogs on a wheel; they always angle toward the center of the curve. To keep the stitches in the correct location requires constant adjustment of the presser foot and fabric. The best method is lift and turn. In this method, you break the curve into a series of short lines of sewing. The key to this method is to never turn the fabric while sewing. On approaching the curve, stop with the needle lowered in the fabric. Lift the presser foot and turn the fabric slightly to make the curve. Sew straight for a stitch or two, then repeat the lift and turn step. This method is the most accurate and assures the best results. I always use it on small, tight curves.

For the best curves, pivot on the correct side of the curve. On outside curves stop and pivot with the needle on the outside of the curves. On inside curves stop and pivot with the needle on the inside of the curve. Stopping and pivoting on the wrong side of the curve causes gaps in the stitching.

Advanced Methods: The lift and turn method for curves is extremely accurate and great on tiny curves. It is also time consuming and unnecessary on larger curves. For the more practiced stitcher, I recommend a method I call "scooting." Scooting is turning the fabric while sewing. It takes some skill to develop the feel for this method. It appears deceptively simple. It is so easy to turn the fabric while stitching. The trick is

in keeping the stitches perpendicular to the edge of the appliqué.

A common mistake with scoot-ing is misaligned stitches. Fig. 6-8 shows the difference between well-placed stitches and incorrectly placed stitches. The wrong stitches happen when the fabric is not being turned enough

to match the curve of the appliqué. The misaligned stitches weaken the appliqué. Two things improve skill levels at scooting curves: sewing at a moderate speed and using a shorter stitch length. These make a smoother curve and help reduce the occurrence of misplaced stitches.

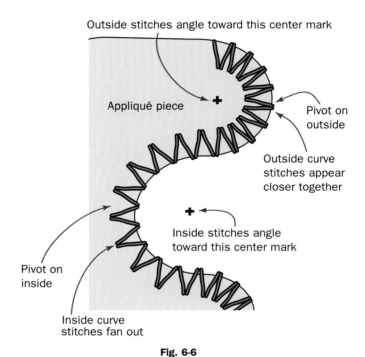

Outside stitches angle toward this center mark

Appliqué piece

Pivot on outside

Outside curve stitches appear closer together

Inside stitches angle toward this center mark

Pivot on inside

Inside curve stitches fan out

Fig. 6-6

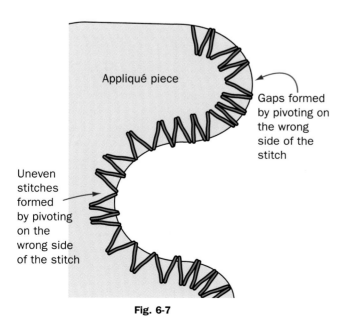

Appliqué piece

Gaps formed by pivoting on the wrong side of the stitch

Uneven stitches formed by pivoting on the wrong side of the stitch

Fig. 6-7

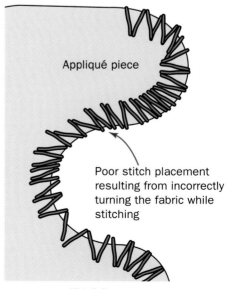

Appliqué piece

Poor stitch placement resulting from incorrectly turning the fabric while stitching

Fig. 6-8

OUTSIDE 90°-OR-GREATER CORNERS

1. Stitch to the very outside point of the corner. The needle should stop at the point in its right hand swing (see Fig. 6-9). Stop with the needle lowered into the background fabric. If the last stitch is going to overshoot the corner, gently hold the fabric back to reduce the forward feed, and force the needle to stop at the corner (see Fig. 6-10).

2. Lift the presser foot and pivot the fabric to make the corner.

3. Lower the presser foot and resume stitching, securing the corner with double stitching.

Broderie perse sample I made to practice stitching greater-than-90° corners.

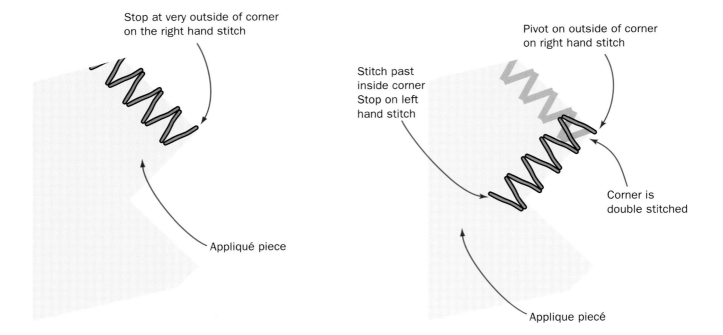

Stop at very outside of corner on the right hand stitch

Appliqué piece

Fig. 6-9

Pivot on outside of corner on right hand stitch

Stitch past inside corner Stop on left hand stitch

Corner is double stitched

Applique piecé

Fig. 6-10

INSIDE 90°-OR-GREATER CORNERS

1 Double stitch this corner to make a secure inner point.

2 Stitch to the corner *and* stitch past it into the appliqué a stitch or two. Yes, it looks like you've missed the point of the corner. The amount stitched into the appliqué is equal to the width of the zigzag. Stop with the needle lowered in the fabric on the *left* hand swing (see fig. 6-11).

3 Lift the presser foot and pivot the fabric to make the corner.

4 Lower the presser foot and resume stitching. Notice how overstitching the corner has resulted in a double stitched point.

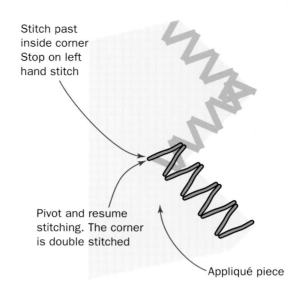

Stitch past inside corner Stop on left hand stitch

Pivot and resume stitching. The corner is double stitched

Appliqué piece

Fig. 6-11

INTRODUCTION TO LESS-THAN-90° CORNERS

The less-than-90° corners are the most difficult of the turns. Sharp corners pose unique problems, although the stitching methods are basically the same as for wider corners. Stitches might extend beyond the appliqué edges as the corners become sharper. To keep the stitches in the correct location requires more pivots and careful placement of the corner stitch. There are a number of suitable methods for turning each corner. Choose the method that works best for you.

 **Sewing Savvy**

Appliqué is easiest on corners of 45° or more. I suggest beginners modify their appliqué patterns to widen all points. The super-sharp points are more difficult to stitch, and are for advanced stitchers.

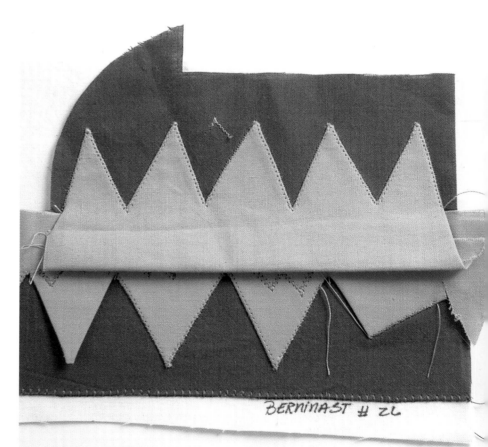

My sample, using scrap fabric, to practice folding and stitching less-than-90° corners.

OUTSIDE LESS-THAN-90° CORNERS, VERSION 1

Double stitch this corner to make a secure outer point. It is best to do so for corners with an angle greater than 45°.

1 Stitch until the left hand stitch falls at the edge of the appliqué (see Fig. 6-12). As you sew, nudge the fabric so that in the right hand stitch you place the needle in the exact corner. The last stitch appears slightly longer than the other stitches. Without nudging, the right hand stitch will fall short of the corner point.

2 The needle should stop in its right hand swing at the point (see Fig. 6-13). Stop with the needle lowered into the background fabric.

3 Lift the presser foot and pivot the fabric to make the corner.

4 Lower the presser foot and resume stitching. Nudge the fabric to ensure the left hand stitch is on the edge of the appliqué piece. The stitch does not extend beyond the appliqué edge. Without nudging, the left hand stitch will fall outside of the appliqué. Note how overstitching the corner has resulted in a double stitched point.

INSIDE LESS-THAN-90° CORNERS, VERSION 1

Double stitch this corner to make a secure inner point (see Fig. 6-14). Stitch the corner using the same steps as the inside-90° corner (see page 58). The corner is secured by a double line of stitching.

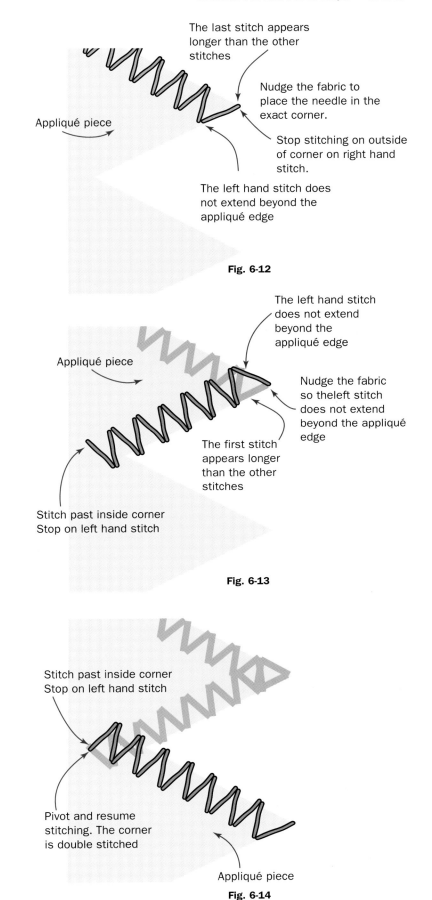

The last stitch appears longer than the other stitches

Nudge the fabric to place the needle in the exact corner.

Appliqué piece

Stop stitching on outside of corner on right hand stitch.

The left hand stitch does not extend beyond the appliqué edge

Fig. 6-12

The left hand stitch does not extend beyond the appliqué edge

Appliqué piece

Nudge the fabric so theleft stitch does not extend beyond the appliqué edge

The first stitch appears longer than the other stitches

Stitch past inside corner
Stop on left hand stitch

Fig. 6-13

Stitch past inside corner
Stop on left hand stitch

Pivot and resume stitching. The corner is double stitched

Appliqué piece

Fig. 6-14

Machine Savvy

USING THE HAND WHEEL TO RAISE OR LOWER THE NEEDLE OR TO MAKE A STITCH

It is important to turn the wheel in the correct direction. On most machines the hand wheel turns toward the front. Turning the hand wheel backwards can cause skipped stitches, broken threads and thread snarls on the bobbin side of the work.

OUTSIDE LESS-THAN-90° CORNERS, VERSION 2

This method is best for corners of less than 45°. It looks identical to the previous corner, but is worked slightly differently.

1 Stitch until the left hand stitch falls at the edge of the appliqué. Stop with the needle lowered in the fabric on the left hand stitch (see Fig. 6-15).

2 Raise the needle out of the fabric. Using the hand wheel, adjust the needle to just above the fabric on the right hand stitch. The needle should not be piercing the fabric.

3 Lift the presser foot. Move the appliqué to place the point of the corner under the needle. The right hand stitch is at the point. Lower the needle into the background fabric. The last stitch appears slightly longer than the other stitches. The amount of adjustment depends on the size of the point. The sharper the point,

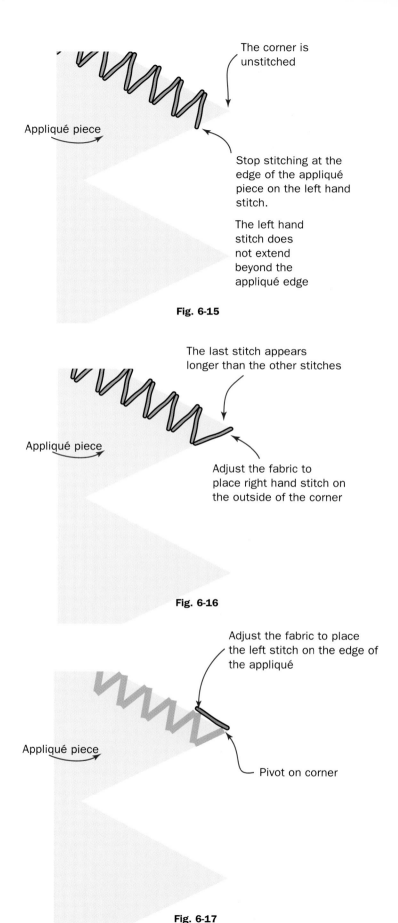

The corner is unstitched

Appliqué piece

Stop stitching at the edge of the appliqué piece on the left hand stitch.

The left hand stitch does not extend beyond the appliqué edge

Fig. 6-15

The last stitch appears longer than the other stitches

Appliqué piece

Adjust the fabric to place right hand stitch on the outside of the corner

Fig. 6-16

Adjust the fabric to place the left stitch on the edge of the appliqué

Appliqué piece

Pivot on corner

Fig. 6-17

the more adjustments are required (see Fig. 6-16).

4 Lift the presser foot and pivot the fabric to turn the corner. Raise the needle out of the fabric. Using the hand wheel, adjust the needle to just above the fabric on the right hand stitch. The needle should not be piercing the fabric.

5 Move the appliqué so the left hand stitch falls at the edge of the appliqué (see Fig. 6-17). I suggest you judge the amount of the move by the last stitch. The stitches on either side of the point should match.

6 Lower the needle into the fabric on the left hand stitch. Adjust the fabric so you can continue stitching along the edge of the appliqué.

7 Lower the presser foot and resume stitching. The corner stitch appears slightly longer than the other stitches.

Advanced Methods: On extremely sharp points there is a small loose triangle of fabric surrounded by stitches at the very point of the corner. This can be corrected by stitching an extra zigzag on the corner point. Stitch to the point of the corner following the basic directions.

1 Stop with the needle lowered at the point in the right hand stitch (see Fig. 6-18). Lift the presser foot and pivot the fabric only half of the turn.

2 Gently hold the fabric to stop it from moving forward and take *two* stitches: one to the left, and one to the right.

3 Stop with the needle lowered in the fabric on the right hand stitch and in the same

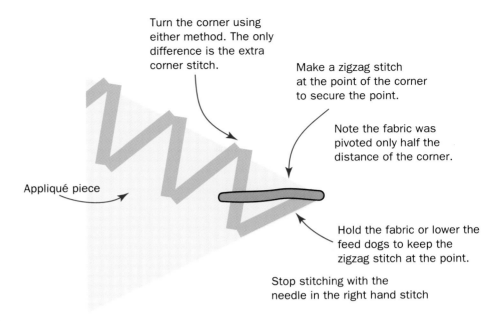

Turn the corner using either method. The only difference is the extra corner stitch.

Make a zigzag stitch at the point of the corner to secure the point.

Note the fabric was pivoted only half the distance of the corner.

Appliqué piece

Hold the fabric or lower the feed dogs to keep the zigzag stitch at the point.

Stop stitching with the needle in the right hand stitch

Fig. 6-18

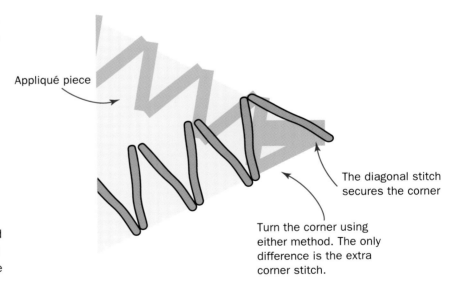

Appliqué piece

The diagonal stitch secures the corner

Turn the corner using either method. The only difference is the extra corner stitch.

Fig. 6-19

needle hole as the previous stitch. The fabric has not moved forward (see Fig. 6-19).

4 Lift the presser foot, pivot the fabric to complete the turn, and resume stitching the corner following basic directions.

INSIDE LESS-THAN-90° CORNERS, VERSION 2

This is a simple open corner; the corner is not secured with double lines of stitching.

1 Stitch to the very (inside) point of the corner. Stop with the needle lowered into the fabric in its right hand swing. The needle is in the valley of the corner.

2 Lift the presser foot and pivot the fabric. Lower the presser foot and resume stitching.

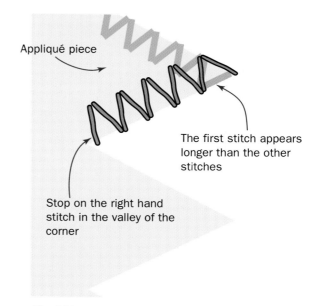

Appliqué piece

The first stitch appears longer than the other stitches

Stop on the right hand stitch in the valley of the corner

Fig. 6-20

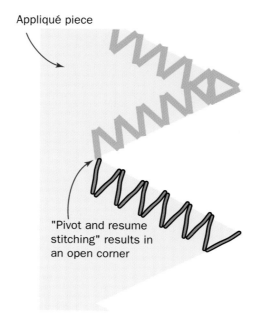

Appliqué piece

"Pivot and resume stitching" results in an open corner

Fig. 6-21

CHAPTER 7
Decorative Stitches for Appliqué

THIS CHAPTER EXPLAINS the basic techniques common to all decorative stitches. Decorative stitches add sparkle and dimension to appliqué. Two basic types of decorative stitches are used:

Duplication of hand stitches: This group includes buttonhole stitch, feather or fly stitch, and stem stitches.

Compact or satin stitches: These stitches, based on satin stitching, result in smooth, filled-in designs. Four common patterns include daisy petals, circles, half circles, and leaf patterns.

THREAD FOR DECORATIVE STITCHES

The list of available sewing and decorative threads is of epic proportions. To simplify the possibilities I will divide the threads into two groups: typical thread choices for all skill levels, and unique thread choices that may appeal to advanced stitchers.

TYPICAL THREAD CHOICES

Machine embroidery threads come in sizes 30, 40, 50, 60, and 80. Machine embroidery thread is as easy to use as regular sewing thread. Fiber choices for machine embroidery thread include rayon, silk, or cotton, and fiber blends like polyester/cotton. Machine embroidery thread is usually thinner, smoother, and glossier than regular sewing thread. Rayon and silk threads are shinier than the cotton threads. Cotton thread is inconspicuous, while rayon or silk thread shows off the stitching. Keep in mind a few things when choosing machine embroidery threads:

❑ The higher the number, the finer the thread.

❑ Choose finer threads for delicate or inconspicuous stitching.

❑ Size 30 thread uses a 12/80 needle.

❑ Size 50 and 60 threads use 11/75 or 12/80 needles.

❑ Size 80 thread uses a 10/70 or 11/75 needle.

Machine Savvy

CHOOSING THE RIGHT NEEDLE FOR THE THREAD

It is a good idea to use the smallest needle size for the thread choice. The smaller needle will make a less conspicuous hole.

There is a simple way to tell if the needle is the right one for the thread. The eye of the needle should be twice the diameter of the thread. No, you don't have to measure the needle eye; judge the needle eye by how easy it is to thread the needle. The thread should go through the needle eye without binding or sticking.

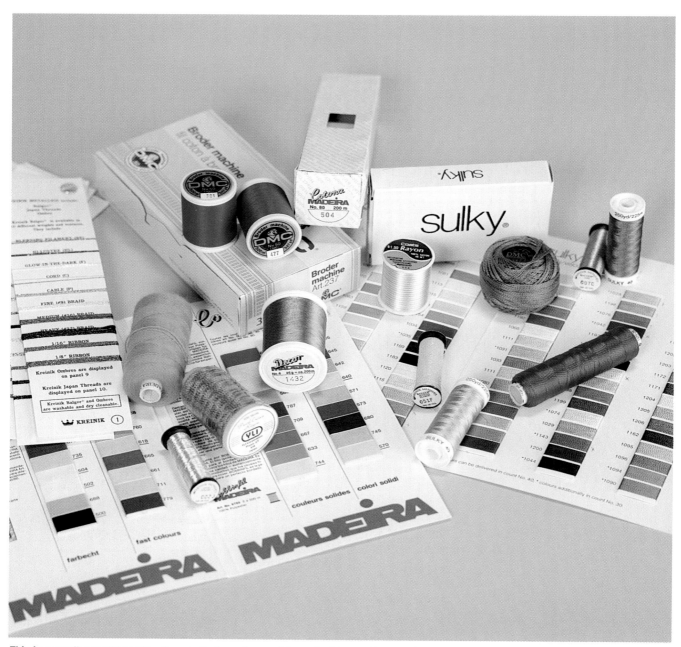

This is a small sampling of the threads that can be used for embroidery and appliqué.

A too small needle size can cause problems. There are two clues that the needle is too small for the thread: the threads fray during stitching, and the machine skips stitches.

Mock Hand Embroidery Floss

One of my favorite thread tricks is using two embroidery threads in the same needle. Two threads give the decorative stitches the look of hand embroidery floss. A single strand of size 30 machine embroidery thread is equal to a single strand of six strand hand embroidery floss. Two threads result in a multi-strand thread that duplicates multiple strands of hand embroidery floss. It's great for blanket stitch and compact decorative stitches. The look is indistinguishable from hand done stitching, plus the heavier threads use a longer stitch length and require less stitching. It is an easy way to add punch to the embroidery stitches and best of all, every machine can handle two threads in a common needle.

Sew A Sample

Decorative Stitching Sample

Supplies

- Two spools of machine embroidery thread, size 30

- Matching thread on the bobbin

- Size 14/90 or 16/100 topstitch needle

What is a topstitch needle?

In a topstitch needle, the eye is twice the size of a regular needle eye. Use a topstitch needle with heavy threads. (Finally, a needle I can thread without bifocals!)

Threading the machine with two threads. Threading the machine with two threads is slightly different from normal threading.

1 To prevent snarls, the thread on one spool should unwind clockwise; the other, counter-clockwise.

2 Place one thread on each side of the tension assembly. Most machines have two sides to the tension assemblies. This ensures even tension on both threads.

3 With one thread, skip the last thread guide on the needle clamp. This prevents the threads from twisting together during stitching and makes the thread look thicker.

4 Place both threads through the eye of the needle. It is easier to thread the needle with both threads at the same time. Smooth the two threads together, and make a fresh cut. Then put both threads through the needle eye, or use a needle threader.

5 Test out the thread and tension. *Sew slowly* until you are sure everything is working correctly. Loosen the top tension if necessary.

Unique Thread Choices

The threads discussed in this section might not work on all machines. They are thicker than regular thread and can require tension adjustments. I have used all of these threads with wonderful results, but they are not for the timid or inexperienced stitcher.

These heavy threads require special handling. You must be willing to experiment with the thread to get the best results. Some threads are used in the needle, while others need to be wound on

a bobbin. You should have an extra bobbin case where you can adjust the tension without affecting other types of sewing. Most of these threads need to be used in the extra bobbin case.

Needle punch yarn: This is a fine acrylic yarn made for use with the fine needle punch. The thread is available from craft stores. It comes on a cardboard core like some serger thread. Because it is a man-made fiber, the colors are brilliant hot reds, oranges, and pinks; bright blues and greens; even eye-popping purples. The white is very white, with a blue tint, compared to the yellow tint of white cotton. I have successfully used this thread in both the needle and the extra bobbin case.

Knitting yarns: For years I have used fine baby yarns and machine knitting yarns on my machine. They work well in the extra bobbin case, but are always slightly heavy looking in the finished project. Needle punch yarn works better and gives better results.

Perle cotton: This is a high luster cotton thread used for hand embroidery and crochet. It is easy to obtain in three sizes: 3, 5, and 8. Size 8, the finest thread, is suitable for either the needle or extra bobbin case. Sizes 5 and 3 are heavier and suitable for only the extra bobbin case.

Rayon, silk, acrylic, or polyester topstitch thread: These threads are traditional choices in clothing construction. The rayon and silk threads have a high luster and are beautiful. The polyester thread is dull by comparison and looks more like hand embroidery floss.

How to Use Novelty Threads in the Needle

When you are using novelty threads in the needle, a topstitch needle is an absolute requirement. I suggest a selection of topstitch needles ranging from sizes 14/90 to 20/120. I most frequently use size 16/100.

Thread the needle as usual. I do recommend loosening the top tension at least one number to accommodate the heavier thread. I also recommend using cotton embroidery thread size 30, or a polyester sewing thread, in the bobbin case. Choose a bobbin thread the same color as the top thread. The top thread usually pulls a dot of bobbin thread to the fabric's right side. The top thread conceals the matching bobbin thread.

Always use an embroidery foot. The cutout on the sole of the foot allows the extra layer of thread to move smoothly. If the machine skips stitches while sewing, try using a regular embroidery foot rather than the open toe embroidery foot.

HOW TO USE NOVELTY THREADS IN THE BOBBIN CASE

Using decorative thread in the bobbin case requires sewing from the wrong side of the work. The bobbin thread is the thread you want on the right side of the quilt.

1 Always use the extra bobbin case. I suggest marking the case latch with a dot of nail polish, but keep the dot small. A heavy or misplaced dot of polish can affect the formation of the stitches.

2 Wind the bobbin by hand, or as a better choice, use the machine's bobbin winder. Place the novelty thread on a thread stand or in an empty jar (I use a peanut butter jar). Place the bobbin on the machine, but don't thread the tension assembly or thread

guides of the bobbin winder. Your fingers take the place of the tension assembly and thread guides. Hold the thread taut and keep it smoothly filling the bobbin while you slowly run the machine. Don't overfill the bobbin.

3 Place the bobbin in the extra case and adjust the tension. The tension adjustment is easiest to explain by comparing it to the regular bobbin case. Thread a full bobbin of sewing thread in the regular bobbin case. Pull on the thread where it comes out of the bobbin. Notice the amount of tension on the thread. Now pull on the novelty thread in the extra bobbin case. Is the tension tighter or looser than the regular thread and bobbin case? Using a small screw driver to adjust

the tension, turn the screw in quarter turns. Remember "righty tighty, lefty loosey." When the tension feels comparable to the normal tension, make a trial line of stitching. Make any further tension adjustments, if necessary.

GENERAL STITCHING INFORMATION FOR DECORATIVE STITCHES

ADJUSTING THE SIZE OF THE STITCHES

Adjust both width and length of the stitches to achieve the desired results. Make the width adjustment using the stitch width dial and double needle feature. The machine's maximum zigzag width

Basic stitch

Shortened using fine thread and stitch length

Lengthened using double thread and stitch length

Lengthened with stitch length only

Lengthened with elongation feature on computerized machines

Fig. 7-1

limits the stitch width. A number of choices affect the stitch length or the length of the pattern repeat.

Stitch length dial. The most common way to change the stitch length is to use the stitch length dial. This method lengthens the stitch by expanding or lengthening the space between the stitches in the pattern.

Thread weights. A second method combines stitch length with differing thread weights. For a short stitch repeat use fine thread and a short stitch length. For longer stitch repeats use a thick thread, or double threads and a longer stitch length. This method is extremely successful on non-computerized machines.

Elongation setting. The third method uses the elongation setting on the machine. Most computerized machines allow the user to lengthen the pattern repeat without affecting the space between the individual stitches. Elongation lengthens the pattern by adding stitches to the pattern repeat, rather than lengthening the space between the stitches (see Fig. 7-1).

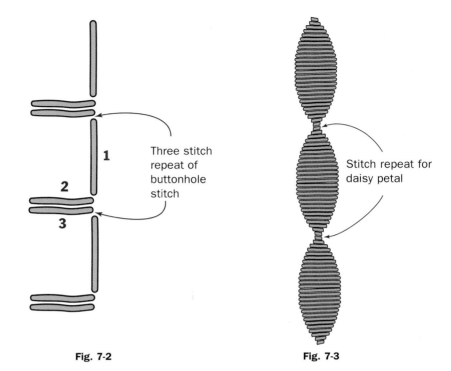

Fig. 7-2

Three stitch repeat of buttonhole stitch

Fig. 7-3

Stitch repeat for daisy petal

Machine Savvy

WHAT IS STITCH REPEAT OR PATTERN REPEAT?

The stitch or pattern repeat is the basic number of stitches in the decorative design stitch. A simple design stitch like the buttonhole stitch has a three stitch repeat. A complex design stitch like the daisy petal can have 20 or more stitches in a pattern. The stitch repeat or pattern repeat refers to the individual design and the number of

stitches making up that design. The Single Pattern feature on computerized machines automatically stops stitching after one pattern repeat.

SECURING THE THREAD TAILS

An important technical consideration in using decorative stitches is beginning and ending each stitching line. Stitches must be secure and inconspicuously knotted. The type of knot chosen depends on the weight of thread and the stitch used.

The simplest knot consists of three or four short straight stitches. Programmed into most computerized machines is a straight stitch knot or "tie off" knot that happens automatically at the beginning and end of the pattern. On less sophisticated machines, make the knot by adjusting the stitch width to straight stitch. Choose this knot for compact stitches based on satin stitch.

Another option is hand knot-

ting the thread tails at both the beginning and end of a stitching line. Leave long thread tails at both the start and finish of the stitching line. Using a hand sewing needle or fine crochet hook, pull the needle threads to the back of the block and tie the bobbin and top threads together to make a square knot. If you are unsure of your knotting skills, use a dot of Fray Check. Hand knotting is the least conspicuous way to knot the straight stitch-based embroidery stitches like buttonhole, feather, and stem stitches. This method is also suitable for heavy novelty threads like yarn and perle cotton.

KEYS TO MATCHING THE DECORATIVE STITCHING TO THE APPLIQUÉ PIECES OR SPACES

Decorative stitching is a sophisticated skill. It requires basic knowledge of how to turn corners and curves, plus how to fit the stitches to the appliqué pieces or spaces. Figure 7-4 shows a common

Detail of Woven Basket block from *Floral Urns* quilt, showing decorative stitches on appliqué pieces.

problem when approaching an appliqué corner; the last pattern repeat is too close to the corner, but an additional pattern repeat will extend beyond the corner. The same problem applies to joining a previous line of stitching (see Fig. 7-5). As anyone who has tried this can tell you, a fix doesn't happen automatically. There isn't a button on the machine that insures perfect results. This skill is not a science. There aren't strict rules or infallible steps. Matching the stitches to the shape of the piece is part practice, part feel, and a little luck. Don't panic! It is not difficult to learn and it is comforting to know that small inconsistencies don't show on the finished appliqué.

1 Always begin stitching at the start of a pattern repeat.

 Hot Tip

Use the machine's pattern begin and single pattern features to accurately start and end a stitch repeat. If your machine doesn't have pattern begin, stitch on scrap fabric to reach the beginning of the pattern repeat.

2 Always use an open toe embroidery foot.

3 A beginner might choose to mark the space required for each pattern by using a stitch ruler. This is an old machine embroidery trick that works like magic.

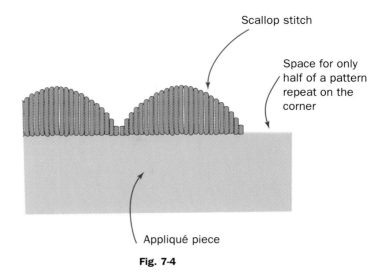

Scallop stitch

Space for only half of a pattern repeat on the corner

Appliqué piece

Fig. 7-4

Appliqué fabric

Scallop stitch

Not enough room for a full stitch repeat when joining a previous line of stitching

Fig. 7-5

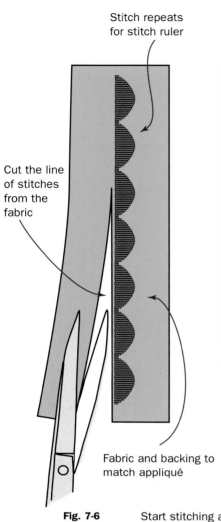

Stitch repeats for stitch ruler

Cut the line of stitches from the fabric

Fabric and backing to match appliqué

Fig. 7-6

Sewing Savvy

To correctly mark corner pattern repeats requires a stitch ruler. The ruler is a line of sample stitching. Stitch a 5" line of sample stitching on a scrap of fabric. Use fabric, backing, and threads identical to the real block to make the sample. After stitching, cut the line of stitches from the sample fabric. Using the sample line of stitching as a ruler, mark five to seven repeats before the corner.

When possible, start sewing at least 2" before the marks. As you approach the corner marks, the stitched patterns might not line up with the marks. That's OK. There are five to seven pattern repeats to correlate the stitches and the marks, and only the last pattern and mark are extremely important. To line up the patterns *gently* affect the feed of the fabric by holding the fabric or pulling on the fabric. The key word is *gently*. It is very easy to over-compensate and move the fabric too much. By the last stitch repeat the pattern and the mark must line up.

This trick works excellently when joining a previous line of stitching. Make the marks five to seven pattern repeats before the starting stitch.

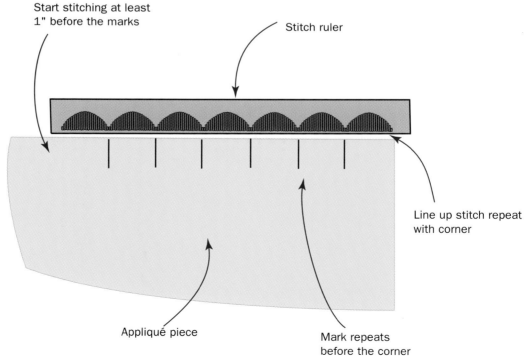

Start stitching at least 1" before the marks

Stitch ruler

Line up stitch repeat with corner

Appliqué piece

Mark repeats before the corner

Fig. 7-7

4 After practicing a few times with measured corners, move on to a more advanced method of judging the spacing by "eye." "Eye" is simply guessing the correct placement of the pattern repeats. This skill simplifies the measure method of turning corners. Don't be dismayed when the first few corners don't look the best. Skill levels improve rapidly with practice.

CIRCLE MAKER

Recently, I made a Sunbonnet Girl quilt that had an antique baby buggy featured on one block. The buggy had two 4" diameter wheels done in a 6.0 width satin stitch. To look correct, the wheels had to be perfectly round, but true embroidered rounds are next to impossible to stitch. The circle maker solved the problem; it always makes perfect circles.

A circle maker is an accessory that fits most brands of machines. I suggest investing in this accessory if you're planning on doing numerous circles. For an occasional circle, make a circle maker using a thumbtack, vinyl tape, and a soft pink eraser. This method lacks the sophistication and simplicity of the machine accessory, but works on the same principle. A sharp point, directly to the left of needle serves as a pivot point for the fabric. The fabric, skewered by the point, pivots in a circle while you are stitching.

A circle maker works with any stitch: satin stitch, straight stitch, even decorative stitches like buttonhole or daisy petals. Fit decorative stitches perfectly to the circle by adjusting the stitch length of the pattern repeat. Best of all, the method is so simple a child could do the stitching and turn out a perfect circle every time.

I give directions for the thumbtack circle maker. For directions for installation and use of the machine accessory, consult the machine dealer.

Sew A Sample

CIRCLE SAMPLE

Supplies

• A sharp, fine point thumbtack with a flat head

• Vinyl tape at least 1" wide

• A new soft pink or white pencil eraser. The eraser is the block type measuring about 2" x 1".

• A six or twelve inch ruler

• 18" square of cotton fabric backed with freezer paper. Mark the center point of each circle on the fabric. Do not mark the circle edge.

Machine Setup

Choose any stitch with the appropriate stitch width and length.

Use the appropriate presser foot for the stitch.

SETTING UP THE CIRCLE MAKER

1 Determine the size of the circle. For the best results, the diameter of the circle should fall between 1" and 16". For Figure 7-8, I used a 3" diameter circle.

2 Determine the radius of the circle. The radius is one half the diameter. The radius of my 3" circle is $1\frac{1}{2}$".

3 Cut a piece of tape at least 1" x 2". From the sticky side, push the thumbtack through the center of the tape rectangle. Set aside the thumbtack and tape.

4 Raise the presser foot and lower the machine needle into the needle hole opening.

5 Place the ruler to the left of the needle and presser foot. Slide the short edge of the ruler against the needle. Adjust the ruler so the very corner, starting at zero, is against the needle and the long straight edge of the ruler is perpendicular to the presser foot. If desired, lower the

My scrap fabric sample to practice making curves using decorative stitches and the circle maker.

presser foot to help hold the ruler in place.

6 Locate the measurement of the radius on the ruler. For this example, locate the 1½" mark (see Fig. 7-8). Place the tape and thumbtack over this mark. The thumbtack point is up, and the sticky side of the tape is against the machine. Lightly press the tape to the machine, not the ruler. Slide the ruler out of the way. Firmly press the remaining tape and the thumbtack to the machine bed.

7 Place the fabric right side up under the presser foot. Place the circle center directly over the thumbtack and press down to force the thumbtack through the freezer paper backing and fabric. Cover the thumbtack point with the eraser. Lightly place the eraser in place. Its only purpose is to shield you from the sharp point of the tack, but the eraser can adversely affect the feed of the fabric if is it too tight against the fabric.

8 Begin stitching. Help smooth the fabric from the thumbtack toward the foot while stitching to ensure a true circle. Use a light touch. If the fabric is sticking or binding on the thumbtack, or causing a hole in the circle center, try a different tack.

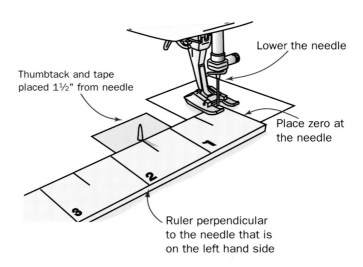

Fig. 7-8

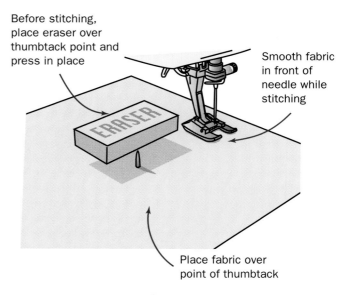

Fig. 7-9

Advanced Methods: The following are ideas to help fit the pattern repeats to the circle:

Make a sample. Always make at least one sample circle before working on the real block. Stitch the circle using the desired circle size with your preferred stitch settings. Note how the pattern repeat fits the circle. This sample gives clues to adjusting the pattern repeat.

Use a stitch ruler. For small inconsistencies, use the stitch ruler as described in Keys to Matching the Stitching to the Appliqué Pieces or Spaces, on page 67. This is the method I use for most decorative stitches. It works extremely well with the buttonhole stitch.

Change stitch length. For larger inconsistencies, or to change the number of repeats, lengthen or shorten the stitch length to adjust the pattern repeat. Remember, a very small adjustment in stitch length can make a large difference when stitching multiple pattern repeats. I use this method only when working with complex patterns

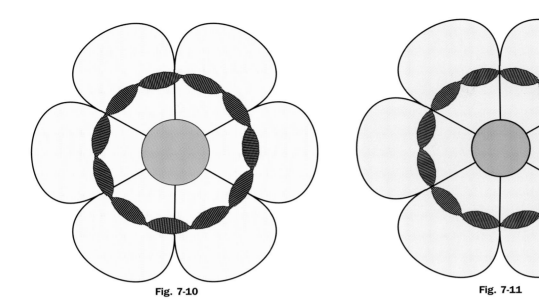

Fig. 7-10   **Fig. 7-11**

like compact stitches. The method helps me increase or reduce the number of pattern repeats in the circle. For example, in Figure 7-10, there are only eleven daisy pattern repeats around the circle. I would prefer twelve pattern repeats to match the six petals of the flower (see Fig. 7-11). To do this requires shortening the stitch length which adds an additional pattern repeat.

Detail of Scallop Basket block from *Floral Urns* quilt, showing use of buttonhole stitch.

Chapter 8
The Buttonhole Stitch

THE BUTTONHOLE STITCH is the most commonly used decorative stitch in appliqué. It can be part of the embellishment of the finished appliqué or, more commonly, a functional stitching used to hold the appliqué to the background. Historically, there are two forms of buttonhole stitch: a small functional stitch and a bold decorative stitch.

The tiny buttonhole stitches are used in broderie perse quilts to secure the raw edges of the motifs. Frequently, the stitching was done using fine white sewing thread on all colors of appliqué. In many respects this is a logical choice. The motifs were always multicolored. The background was usually white or cream. Choosing a thread to match the background precluded the changing of threads to match the individual colors of the motifs.

The other form of buttonhole stitch was popular during the 1930s. Traditionally, this bold, heavy stitching has been called blanket stitching. Usually a black or dark embroidery floss was used to stitch on all colors of appliqué. This large-scale, high-contrast stitching requires precise placement of individual stitches for attractive corners and curves.

Buttonhole stitch has at least four other names: blanket stitch, point de Paris, pin stitch, and single hem stitch. No matter the name, the basic elements of the stitch are the same: straight stitches divided by a zigzag that is *not* feeding forward. Note that the zigzag stitch is perpendicular to the straight stitch line (see Fig. 8-1). Only perpendicular stitches are capable of turning complex corners. More limited in use are the buttonhole stitches with angled zigzag.

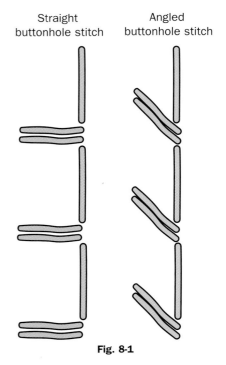

Straight buttonhole stitch   Angled buttonhole stitch

Fig. 8-1

There are two ways to make a buttonhole stitch: single-stitched buttonhole stitch and multiple-stitched buttonhole stitch. The single-stitched buttonhole stitch is a forward moving stitch. Every portion of this stitch is a single line of thread. It is easier to control on the corners and curves and is the best choice for the fine stitches of broderie perse. In the multiple-stitched buttonhole stitch, the fabric moves forward and backward so every stitch is oversewn at least two times. The multiple-stitched buttonhole stitch looks thicker and more like the hand embroidery thread used in decorative stitching.

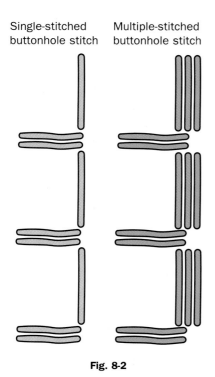

Single-stitched buttonhole stitch   Multiple-stitched buttonhole stitch

Fig. 8-2

Sew A Sample

SINGLE-STITCHED BUTTONHOLE STITCH FOR BRODERIE PERSE SAMPLE

Set up your sewing machine to try the two basic stitches. Start by practicing the single-stitched buttonhole stitch.

Supplies

• Fine white or cream machine embroidery thread size 50 or size 60, or fine machine embroidery thread to match the background fabric

• Size 10/70 or 11/75 machine needle

• Scrap of white cotton backed with freezer paper

Machine Setup

Single-stitched buttonhole stitch

Stitch width 1.0 to 1.5

Stitch length 1.0 to 1.5

BASIC BOLD BUTTONHOLE OR BLANKET STITCH

Make the basic bold buttonhole stitch or blanket stitch using a single-stitched buttonhole stitch. The single-stitched buttonhole stitch can be made thicker by using two threads in the needle. That way it looks like it was made with hand embroidery floss. The straight stitch will have two threads; the zigzag, four threads. As a result the stitching appears to be three strands of hand embroidery thread.

The large scale of the stitches affects how securely the appliqué is held in place. Blanket stitching is functional for appliqué pieces that have folded edges. For raw edge appliqué the distance between the stitches is too large to secure the appliqué and prevent the raw edges from fraying. For raw edges use a small invisible zigzag as the functional stitching, and embroider over the finished edges with the decorative buttonhole stitching.

Sew A Sample

BOLD BUTTONHOLE OR BLANKET STITCH SAMPLE

Now set up your sewing machine to try making a bold buttonhole stitch.

Supplies

• Two spools of black or other contrasting machine embroidery thread size 30

• Matching thread in the bobbin

• Size 14/90 or 16/100 topstitch needle

• Scrap of white cotton backed with freezer paper

Machine Setup

Single-stitched buttonhole stitch

Stitch width 3.0 to 5.5

Stitch length 3.5 to 6.0

Thread the machine with two size 30 machine embroidery threads in the needle.

USING THE BUTTONHOLE STITCH

There are many parts to mastering machine buttonhole stitching. That's why I'm always perplexed by the buttonhole directions that imply all I must do is choose the stitch and sew. These directions ignore a dozen questions about the nuts and bolts of the stitch. How do I start? How do I turn corners? How do I make the last stitch match the first when I join a previous row of stitching? How do I get the stitches to fit the corners? This section will answer those questions and many more. (See photo below.)

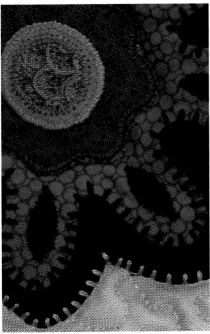

Detail of Scallop Basket block, showing buttonhole stitches.

TURNING CORNERS WITH THE BUTTONHOLE STITCH

The most basic skill in using the buttonhole stitch is in turning corners and curves. No matter what scale stitch you choose for your project, for buttonhole-stitch corners and curves you have to follow very specific steps to make precise stitches.

There are two parts to making successful corners and curves. First is mastering the basic steps of each type of corner or curve. This is knowing how to turn each of the four corners and two curves. Second is fitting the basic steps to the appliqué piece.

The best way to practice corners and curves is by dividing the skills into its parts. First, practice

the corners and curves, and second, practice fitting them to the appliqué pieces.

The directions in the next section will explain the basic steps of each type of corner and curve.

 Sew A Sample

TURNING CORNERS AND CURVES SAMPLE

Supplies

- Two 18" squares of light-colored cotton fabric backed with freezer paper

- Open toe embroidery foot

- A dark or bright colored thread. Any type of thread will work for the samples.

Machine Setup

Single-stitched buttonhole stitch

Medium stitch width

Medium stitch length

(I recommend medium settings for trying a sample. You can adjust more exact settings in later steps.)

The best method for learning how to turn corners and curves with the buttonhole stitch is to practice on a single layer of fabric. At this point you are just practicing the steps to turning the corners and curves. There are no marks, guides, or appliqué pieces on the background fabric.

The basic instructions use a simple single-stitched buttonhole stitch (see Fig. 8-1). The stitch should zigzag to the left. You may need to choose lateral mirror imaging to have a left swing stitch (see page 9).

 Machine Savvy

RIGHT VERSUS LEFT SWING OF THE ZIGZAG STITCH

Like all appliqué stitches, buttonhole stitches have a right hand or left hand orientation. Sew clockwise around the appliqué pieces when the straight stitches are on the right and the zigzag stitches to the left. This is right-handed stitching. Sew counterclockwise around the appliqué when the straight stitches are on the left and the zigzag stitches to the right. This is left handed stitching.

The basic corner and curve directions are for right handed clockwise stitching. If your machine has only a left hand counterclockwise stitch, simply reverse the turns. When the directions state, "Turn clockwise," you will turn your fabric counterclockwise. Thankfully, this is harder to write than it is to do!

1 Stitch all buttonhole stitch corners and curves with basically the same method. Later sections will discuss turning curves and corners with multi-stitched buttonhole stitches.

2 Thread the bobbin and needle with matching thread.

3 Slightly loosen the top tension. For in-depth directions on how to adjust the top tension, see page 54 in Chapter 6, Invisibly Stitching the Appliqué.

90° INSIDE AND OUTSIDE CORNERS

Ninety-degree corners are the easiest. You stitch a line of steps as shown in Figure 8-3. Half the corners are outside corners; half are inside corners. I have marked the inside and outside corners to help you identify what your sample should look like.

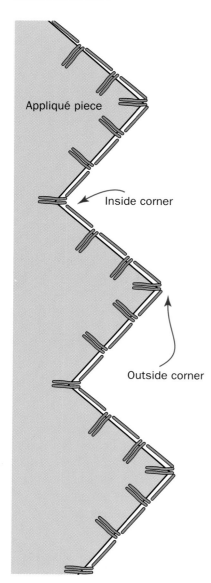

Appliqué piece

Inside corner

Outside corner

Fig. 8-3

90°-OR-LARGER OUTSIDE CORNERS

This is a two step corner. The corner requires that you lift the presser foot twice. Lift the first time when you turn half the corner. This stitch forms the diagonal stitch at the point of the corner. Then you lift again when you make a second turn that completes the corner.

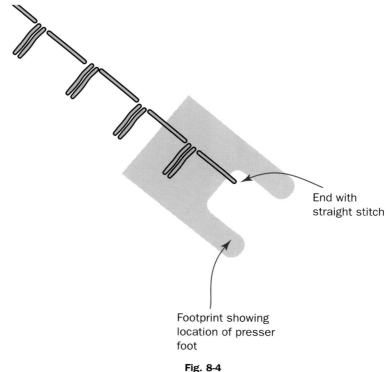

End with straight stitch

Footprint showing location of presser foot

Fig. 8-4

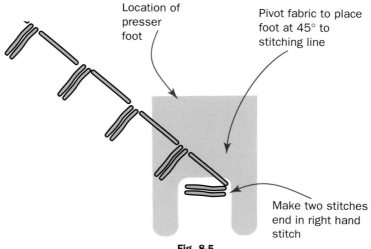

Location of presser foot

Pivot fabric to place foot at 45° to stitching line

Make two stitches end in right hand stitch

Fig. 8-5

1 Begin any place on your fabric. Stitch a few stitches, ending with the straight stitch (see Fig. 8-4).

2 The next stitch you will be taking is the zigzag. Lower the needle in the fabric. Pivot the fabric counterclockwise 45° (see Fig. 8-5). That is one half of the 90° corner.

Machine Savvy

WHAT IS A COUNTER-CLOCKWISE TURN?

Imagine that the fabric is the face of a clock and the needle is in the exact center of the face. To pivot the fabric counterclockwise, push the right side of the fabric away from you, bringing the left side toward you. A clockwise pivot is the opposite.

3 Make *two* zigzag stitches, one to the left and one to the right. Lower the needle into the fabric in its right hand swing, *and* in the same needle hole as the previous stitch. The fabric has not moved forward.

4 Lift the presser foot and pivot the fabric the second last half of the turn. Lower the presser foot and resume stitching.

Do your corner stitches look like Figure 8-7? Stitch width and length affect the stitch placement in the corners. In the perfect corner, the stitches do not overlap. They can be very close together, even touching, but never overlapping. To correct the problem, narrow the stitch width and/or lengthen the stitch length. As a general rule, the stitch length should be equal to or greater than the stitch width. I usually have the stitch length .5mm longer than the stitch width. This ratio is applicable to any size buttonhole stitch. Before you choose a width and length for your stitches, make a sample corner to ensure you have the correct ratio.

The buttonhole stitch can be in any size from the tiny stitches

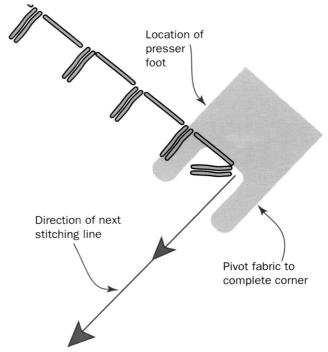

Location of presser foot

Direction of next stitching line

Pivot fabric to complete corner

Fig. 8-6

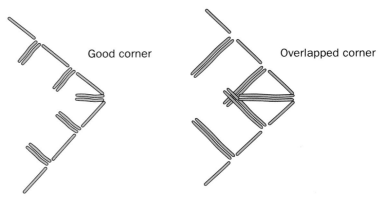

Good corner

Overlapped corner

Fig. 8-7

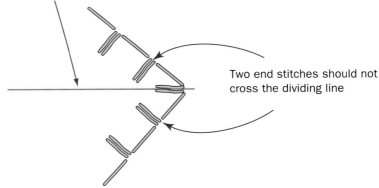

Imaginary line dividing the corner in half

Two end stitches should not cross the dividing line

Fig. 8-8

of broderie perse to the large ones of blanket stitching. Determine the stitch size by the size of the appliqué pieces and the look you are trying to achieve. Here is a list of possible stitch sizes for buttonhole stitching:

Width	Length
1.0	1.5
1.5	2.0
2.0	2.5
2.5	3.0
3.0	3.5
3.5	4.0
4.0	4.5
4.5	5.0

90°-OR-LARGER INSIDE CORNERS

This is a two step corner. The corner requires that you lift the presser foot twice. Lift the first time when you turn half the corner. This stitch forms the diagonal stitch at the point of the corner. Lift the second time when you turn again to complete the corner.

Note: *Turn this corner in the opposite direction of the outside corner.*

1 Stitch about seven stitches, ending with the straight stitch (see Fig. 8-9).

2 The next stitch you will be taking is the zigzag. Lower the needle in the fabric. Pivot the fabric clockwise 45°. That is one half of the 90° corner.

3 Make *two* zigzag stitches, one to the left and one to the right. Lower the needle into the fabric in its right hand swing *and* in the same needle hole as the previous stitch. The fabric has not moved forward (see Fig. 8-10).

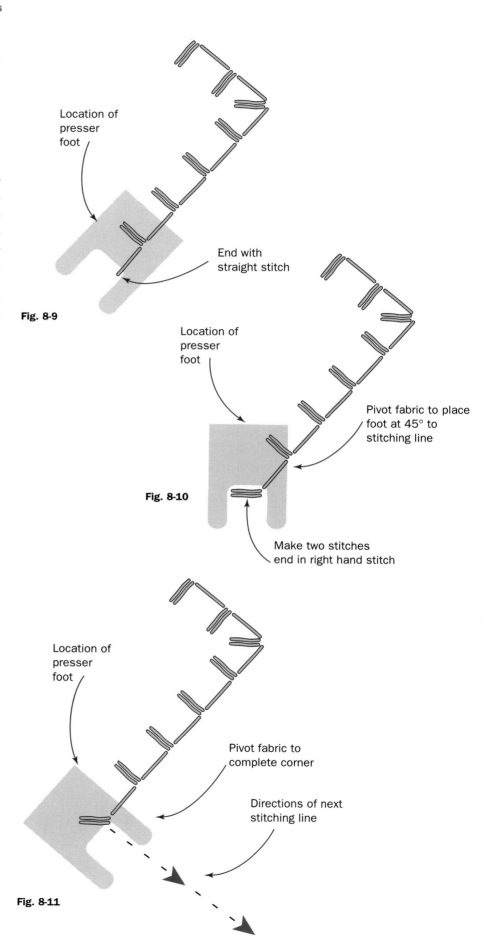

Location of presser foot

End with straight stitch

Fig. 8-9

Location of presser foot

Pivot fabric to place foot at 45° to stitching line

Fig. 8-10

Make two stitches end in right hand stitch

Location of presser foot

Pivot fabric to complete corner

Directions of next stitching line

Fig. 8-11

4 Lift the presser foot and pivot the fabric the second half of the turn. Lower the presser foot and resume stitching (see Fig. 8-11).

To practice making 90° corners, alternate inside and outside corners to make a row of stitching that looks like stair steps.

LESS-THAN-90° OUTSIDE CORNERS

Sharp outside points are the most difficult part of buttonhole stitching. The smaller the stitch width, the less difficult it is to turn these corners. Bold buttonhole or blanket stitching are the hardest to master. I recommend bold buttonhole or blanket stitching for corners that are at least a 45° angle. Figure 8-12 shows a 45° turn.

Basically, stitch the sharp points of these corners like the wider corners. It is a two step corner where you lift the presser foot twice. The first turn is the stitch that forms the diagonal stitch at the point of the corner. The second turn completes the corner. Figure 8-13 shows what happens when you apply the basic directions to the sharp point of the corner. The stitches at the corners overlap. On extremely fine points the stitches may sew completely across the point. Either way the results are a messy corner.

The best way to understand how to stitch the corner is to study well-done samples of sharp corners. Look closely at Figure 8-12. Note how the zigzag stitches meet just before the point. If you were to draw a line dividing the point in half, you would see that the stitches on the sides of the corner must not cross the center line. On sharp points the distance between the last side zigzag stitch and the point zigzag stitch is longer than the basic stitch length. The corner

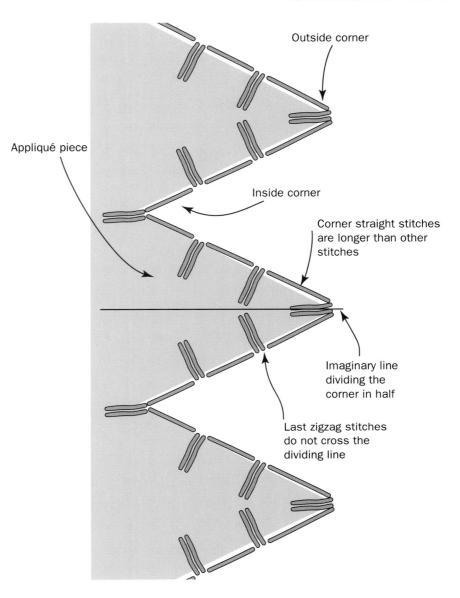

Outside corner

Appliqué piece

Inside corner

Corner straight stitches are longer than other stitches

Imaginary line dividing the corner in half

Last zigzag stitches do not cross the dividing line

Fig. 8-12

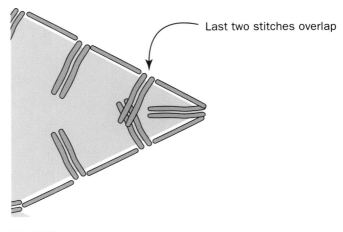

Last two stitches overlap

Fig. 8-13

straight stitch is longer than the distance between other straight stitches. You could lengthen the stitch length to compensate for the space. The better choice is to lift the presser foot and move the fabric so the next stitch is in the correct location. There are at least a dozen successful ways to do this step. I'll explain my method, but you can use any way that gives the correct results.

1 Make the last zigzag before the corner. Stop stitching on the right hand swing. Lower the needle into the fabric.

2 Turn the hand wheel to begin the straight stitch. Stop turning the handwheel just before the needle goes into the fabric.

Machine Savvy

USING THE HAND WHEEL

Use the hand wheel to raise or lower the needle or to make a stitch. It is important to turn the wheel in the correct direction. On most machines the hand wheel turns toward the front. Turning the hand wheel backwards can cause skipped stitches, broken threads and thread snarls on the bobbin side of the work.

3 Lift the presser foot and move the fabric so the needle is directly over the point of the corner. Lower the presser foot and needle to complete the stitch.

4 Pivot the fabric counterclockwise, turning one half of the corner.

5 Make *two* zigzag stitches, one to the left and one to the right. Lower the needle into the fabric in its right hand swing *and* in the same needle hole as the previous stitch. The fabric has not moved forward.

6 Lift the presser foot and pivot the fabric the second half of the turn. The second side of the corner will require a longer straight stitch to match the first side of the corner. Turn the hand wheel to begin the straight stitch. Stop turning the hand wheel just before the needle goes into the fabric. Lift the presser foot and move the fabric the same distance you did on the opposite side. Lower the presser foot and resume stitching.

90°-OR-LESS INSIDE CORNERS

Follow the directions for 90°-or-larger inside corners (see page 80).

INSIDE AND OUTSIDE CURVES

Successful curves require stitches to be perpendicular to the edge of the appliqué. Place the stitches like cogs on a wheel; they should always angle toward the center of the curve. To keep the stitches at the correct angle requires constant adjustment of the presser foot and fabric. The best method is lift and turn.

1 In this method, break the curve into a series of short straight lines. The key to this method is to never turn the fabric as you sew.

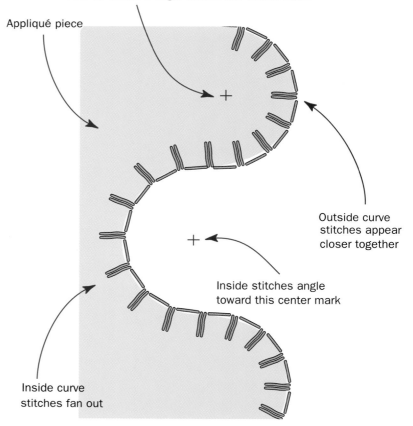

Outside stitches angle toward this center mark

Appliqué piece

Outside curve stitches appear closer together

Inside stitches angle toward this center mark

Inside curve stitches fan out

Fig. 8-14

2 As you approach the curve, stop on a straight stitch section with the needle lowered in the fabric. Lift the presser foot and turn the fabric slightly to make the curve.

3 Sew straight for a stitch or two, then repeat the lift and turn step. This method is the most accurate and assures the best results. I always use it on small tight curves. The key to great looking buttonhole stitch curves is to always pivot on the straight stitch portion of the stitch, never on the zigzag stitch.

USING BUTTONHOLE STITCHES WITH APPLIQUÉ

Stitch placement. The straight stitch portion of the buttonhole stitch should be as close as possible to the edge of the appliqué without stitching into the appliqué piece. Only the zigzag stitches should be on the appliqué.

Starting and stopping a line of stitching. When possible, it is best to start stitching with the straight stitch. On many machines you can use the Pattern Begin or Pattern Start function to ensure that you always begin with the

Scallop Basket block from *Floral Urns* quilt.

same portion of the stitch. Some patterns begin with the zigzag portion of the stitch; this is acceptable. The advantage to the Pattern Begin function is that you know what will be the first stitch.

The buttonhole stitch should be hand knotted at both the beginning and end of a stitching line. Leave long thread tails at both the start and finish of the stitching line. Pull the top threads to the back of the block and tie the bobbin and top threads together to make a secure knot. If you're unsure of your knotting skills, use a dot of Fray Check. Hand knotting is the only acceptable way to knot the bold buttonhole or blanket stitches.

MULTIPLE-STITCHED BUTTONHOLE STITCHES

There are many variations of the multiple-stitched buttonhole stitch. Not all multiple-stitched buttonhole stitches will turn corners or curves successfully. The best stitches complete all the stitches in each section before moving to the next section. Some multiple-stitched buttonhole stitches make one straight stitch *backward* after stitching the zigzag! It is impossible to turn a corner with this type of stitch. If you are in the market for a new machine and want the buttonhole stitch,

check out the stitching sequence.

Multiple-stitched buttonhole stitch corners and curves are made using the same directions as for the single-stitched buttonhole stitch (see page 77), with the exception of less-than-45° corners. Sharp corners require a lengthened straight stitch.

The trick to successfully turning the corners is knowing how many stitches make up each portion of the stitch. Are there three stitches or five stitches to the straight stitch? Are there two stitches or four stitches to the zigzag?

The Single Pattern function may help in turning curves and corners. Make a sample of the buttonhole stitch using the Single Pattern function to determine the end of the pattern. It is great for corners if the pattern ends after the straight portion and before the zigzag stitch. Press Single Pattern as you approach the corner to ensure that you stop at the correct point for the pivot.

FITTING THE STITCHES TO THE APPLIQUÉ PIECE

Buttonhole stitching is a sophisticated skill. It requires basic knowledge of how to turn corners and curves plus how to fit the stitches to the appliqué pieces. Anyone who has tried the machine button-

hole stitch will tell you the true mastery of buttonhole stitching is in having the stitch fit the appliqué.

KEYS TO FITTING THE BUTTONHOLE STITCH TO THE PIECE

❑ The shorter the stitch length, the easier it is to fit the stitching to the appliqué piece.

❑ Always use an open toe embroidery foot.

❑ Using a sample line of stitching as a ruler, mark five to seven stitches before the corner or the join of the stitching lines.

❑ After practicing a few times with measured corners, move on to a more advanced method of judging the spacing by "eye." "Eye" is simply guessing the correct placement of the stitches. This is a skill based on the measure method and skill levels improve rapidly with practice. Plus, there is a way to cheat: small errors are simple to fix, whether the last stitch is too far away or too close to the corner. Simply lift the presser foot and move the fabric to the right spot. A small amount of cheating won't show, and it's better than picking out stitches.

CHAPTER 9
Duplicating Hand Stitches

BASIC BUTTONHOLE STITCH is the most commonly used decorative stitch in appliqué, but there are many other stitches that can duplicate hand embroidery stitches. These stitches are used exclusively for embellishing the appliqué rather than attaching the appliqué pieces to the background.

ANGLED BUTTONHOLE STITCH

This is an advanced method for computerized machines: the angled buttonhole stitch used for feathered-edge appliqué requires that your sewing machine have the lateral and axial mirror imaging features for this stitch, available only on some computerized sewing machines.

The angled buttonhole stitch is a wonderful stitch to use to add detail to the edges of leaves and buds. Placed with the straight stitch along the outer edge of the appliqué piece and the zigzag extending up and outward from the appliqué, the angled buttonhole stitch gives a feathered edge. Because the pattern is a one way design, it is not possible to stitch around a leaf by simply pivoting at the outer or inner point. To use this stitch for a feathered edge requires axial and lateral mirror imaging (see definition on page 9). Figures 9-1 and 9-2 demonstrate the right and left sides of the leaf with and without using axial and lateral mirror imaging.

The leaf can be stitched starting at the leaf base, or at the leaf point (see Fig. 9-3). Starting at the leaf base allows you to stitch the entire leaf in a single line of stitching and with practice is the fastest method of stitching. Starting at the leaf point requires two lines of stitching, one on each side of the leaf, and ensures the best leaf point. Either method works, although I personally prefer starting at the leaf point.

1 Start stitching at the leaf base for a single line of stitching.

2 Stop stitching at the outer point of the leaf and pivot the work.

3 Engage axial mirror imaging to reverse the angle of the stitches. Engage lateral

imaging to reverse the left/right orientation of the stitches.

4 Continue stitching to complete the leaf or bud.

Machine Savvy

HOW DO I TURN CORNERS SUCCESSFULLY WITH THE PIVOT STITCH?

Depending on the machine's features, turning the corner may be most successful when the pivot stitch is on the last stitch of the pattern repeat. On some machines, engaging the mirror imaging will automatically return the pattern to the pattern start. On other machines the pattern will continue stitching from the current stitch. Getting a perfectly balanced corner will require working within the machine's capabilities. Possible methods can include turning half the corner to place the zigzag on the exact point of the leaf or having only straight stitches at the corners.

Successful Corners. Start stitching at the leaf point for the most successful corners. This ensures the point starts at the correct stitch and reduces the chance of "mis-stitches" at the leaf point. Stitch each side of the leaf from point to base. Use axial and lateral mirror imaging to obtain the correct stitch orientation. This ensures a perfect point every time.

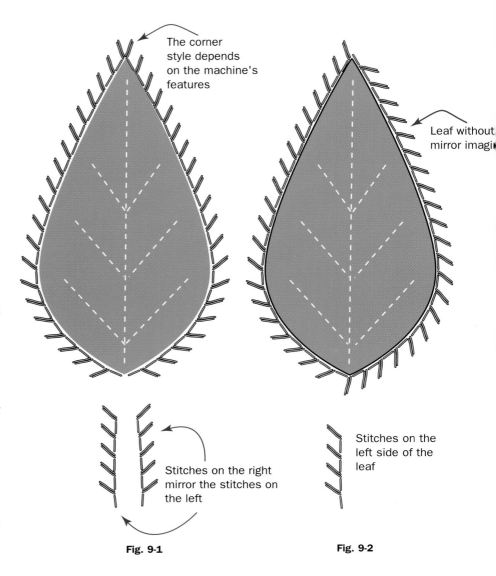

The corner style depends on the machine's features

Leaf without mirror imagi

Stitches on the right mirror the stitches on the left

Stitches on the left side of the leaf

Fig. 9-1

Fig. 9-2

Stitch formation when stitching clockwise around leaf

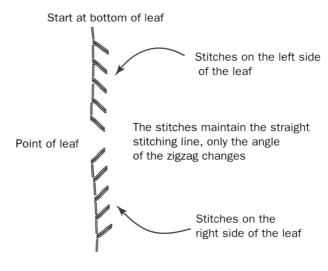

Start at bottom of leaf

Stitches on the left side of the leaf

Point of leaf

The stitches maintain the straight stitching line, only the angle of the zigzag changes

Stitches on the right side of the leaf

End at bottom of leaf   **Fig. 9-3**

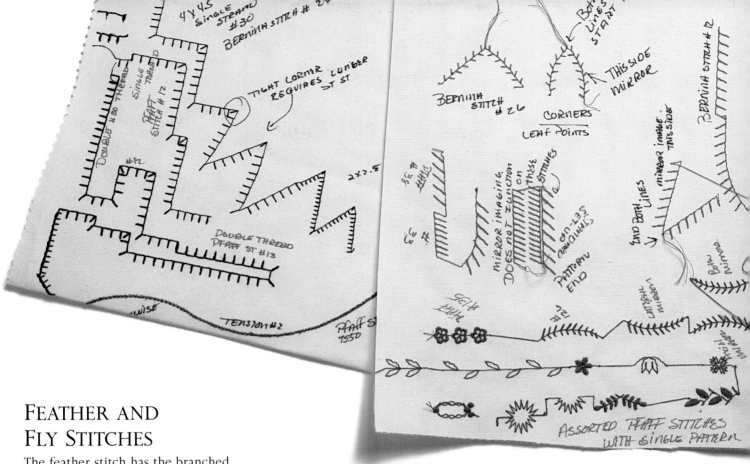

My samples to experiment with duplicating hand stitches.

FEATHER AND FLY STITCHES

The feather stitch has the branched look of a true feather stitch. The fly stitch has very similar branches, but the fly stitch has a straight stitch spine, while the feather

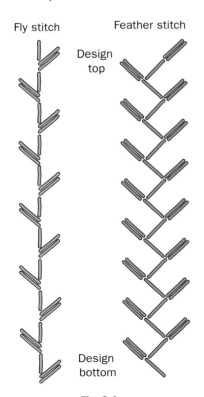

Fly stitch   Feather stitch

Design top

Design bottom

Fig. 9-4

stitch has a zigzag spine. In a true fly stitch, the branches always are in pairs. Machine fly stitches frequently have single alternating branches (see Fig. 9-4). The fly stitch with its straight spine is easier to control on curves than the zigzag-based feather stitch.

Notice that these stitches are one way designs: there is a top and bottom to the stitch. Usually the branches point up or away from the base of a leaf or petal.

USES FOR FEATHER AND FLY STITCHING

Feather and fly stitches are best for adding detailing to leaves and around the edges of simple leaf shapes. Combined with a tapered stitch width, these stitches make great veins in leaves and wonderful fern shaped lines of embroidery. Neither fly nor feather stitch turns sharp corners with the

accuracy of a buttonhole stitch. In comparison, the fly stitch makes a better corner than the feather stitch.

Because the fly stitch is a one-way design, it is not possible to stitch around a leaf by simply pivoting at the outer or inner point. Simple pivoting will reverse the stitches. Without the mirror imaging feature, the leaf will require two lines of stitching to ensure the stitches are at the correct angle. Each line starts at the base of the leaf, stitching toward the point (see Fig. 9-5 on page 88).

If you have a computerized sewing machine and the capability, use axial mirror imaging to invert the direction of the fly stitch and stitch the leaf outline in one line of stitching. At the corner, stop stitching and pivot the work. Engage axial mirror imaging and continue stitching.

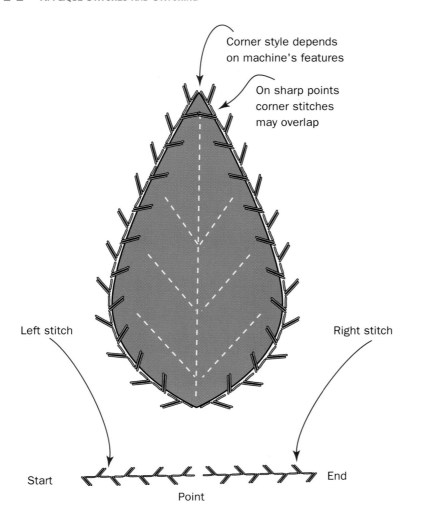

Corner style depends on machine's features

On sharp points corner stitches may overlap

Left stitch

Right stitch

Start

End

Point

Fig. 9-5

Machine Savvy

HOW DO I GET A PERFECTLY BALANCED CORNER WITH FLY AND FEATHER STITCHING?

Depending on the machine's features, turning the corner may be most successful when the pivot stitch is the last stitch of the pattern repeat. On some machines engaging the mirror imaging will automatically return the pattern to the pattern start. On other machines the pattern will continue stitching from the current stitch. Getting a perfectly balanced corner will require working within the machine's capabilities. Possible methods can include turning half the corner to place the zigzag on the exact point of the leaf or having only straight stitches at the corners.

Look for variations of feather and fly stitches. For example, the Pfaff Creative 7550 has a great pattern (number 126), that makes a tapered fly stitch leaf.

Adjust stitch width to omit overlapped stitches

Fig. 9-6

Pfaff Creative 7550 stitch Number 126

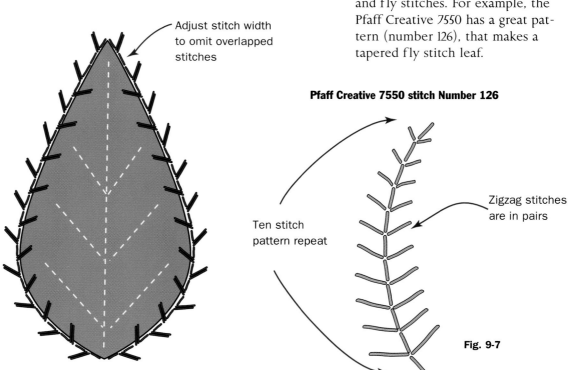

Ten stitch pattern repeat

Zigzag stitches are in pairs

Fig. 9-7

Tapering the fly stitch. This is an advanced method. With practice, you can make your own version of the Pfaff fly stitch using the stitch width control. Just don't expect your tapered fly stitches to be as uniform as the automatic stitch. Make a tapered stitch by varying the stitch width during stitching. Tapering requires a steady hand. The trick is to make a smooth, well-shaped taper—not too short, not too long.

1 Start at the narrowest end of the pattern. The point is the most visible and important part of the pattern. Starting with the point ensures a smooth taper in the allotted space. Set the stitch width at straight stitch.

2 Begin stitching and slowly widen the stitch width while guiding the fabric. Don't look at the stitch width control. Keep focused on the line of stitching. See satin stitch tapering on page 94 for more suggestions on perfecting the taper.

STEM STITCH

This stitch is a straight stitch variation. The machine guides the fabric forward and backward to form an angled line of stitches resembling the handmade stem stitch. Some machines have a single stitched stem, while others have a multiple stitched stem. The multiple stitched stem is heavier and looks more like hand embroidery. Both stitches work equally well. The stitch is designed to curve and loop. There is a trick to making this stitch turn great curves. Figure 9-9 shows the most common stitch formation. This stitch is best for clockwise turns. When you turn against the stitch, the stem becomes wider and looks more like a zigzag. Stem stitch doesn't corner well.

USES FOR STEM STITCH

The most obvious use for the stem stitch is to make fine stems. The stitch also does wonderful looped grape tendrils. It can add dimension to leaves and flowers and can be used to outline the appliqué.

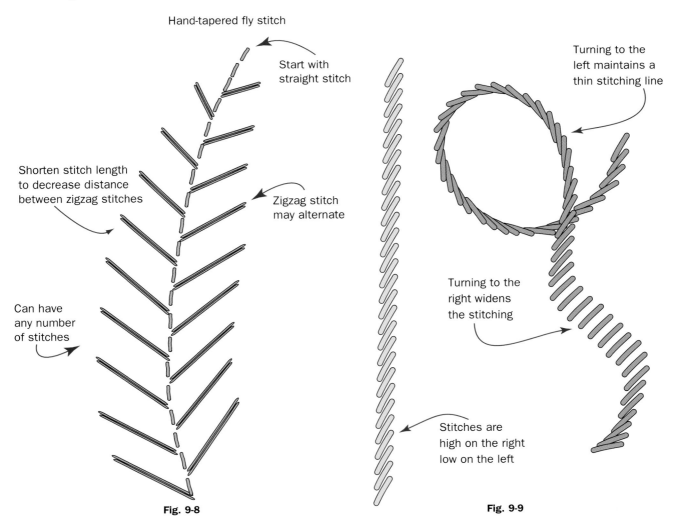

Hand-tapered fly stitch

Start with straight stitch

Shorten stitch length to decrease distance between zigzag stitches

Zigzag stitch may alternate

Can have any number of stitches

Turning to the left maintains a thin stitching line

Turning to the right widens the stitching

Stitches are high on the right low on the left

Fig. 9-8

Fig. 9-9

STRAIGHT STITCH FOR DECORATIVE STITCHING

One of the easiest ways to embellish your appliqué is to use a straight stitch. You don't need a fancy sewing machine—everyone has a straight stitch. Use the straight stitch to stitch the appliqué in place or for embroidering the appliqués.

Straight-stitch appliqué is an old-fashioned way to stitch the appliqué pieces to the background fabric. The method dates to the mid-to-late 1800s when owning a "new" sewing machine was considered prestigious and the owners were eager to show off their prized possession. Choose straight stitch appliqué for simple shape, turned-edge appliqué patterns. The straight stitching is topstitching approximately $1/8$" from the folded edge of the appliqué. I recommend using an edgestitch or topstitch foot to help uniformly guide the stitching around the shape. Options include using decorative threads or doing multiple lines of stitching.

Straight stitch embroidery has a wider range of applications. It can be extremely fine, almost invisible, stitching or bold, high contrast, stitching. Use it to add detail, color, and dimension to the appliqué pieces. For most straight stitch embroidery I recommend free motion stitching. Use the darning foot and lower the feed dogs. Use free motion straight stitch embroidery as you would a fine tip marker. It can outline elements, add shading, draw fine details, or write on the blocks.

CHAPTER 10
Decorative Satin Stitching

SATIN STITCHING ADDS EMBROIDERY to the finished appliqué. Don't confuse decorative satin stitching with the uniform satin stitch edging used to stitch appliqué pieces in place. Decorative satin stitching employs a number of built-in stitches, plus it uses tapering. The tapering combined with a simple satin stitch in varying stitch widths becomes an embellishment for the appliqué. Frequently, decorative satin stitching duplicates traditional motifs added to hand appliquéd pieces.

COMPACT STITCHES

These dramatic and highly visible stitches correspond to handmade satin stitch motifs. All these stitches use a wide stitch width and short stitch length to get smooth, filled-in designs. Use these stitches in appliqué to add texture to the fabrics, or substitute them for tiny portions of appliqué that are too small to cut from fabric. There are dozens of possible patterns. I consistently use four patterns: daisy petals, circles, half circles, and leaves.

Options: There are hundreds of built-in decorative stitches on most machines: stars, leaves, and flowers, as well as a wide selection of graphic designs like Greek keys or step pyramids. Any stitch can be fitted to appliqué. Even utility stitches like the mending stitch can add interest to appliqué. The possibilities are limited only by your imagination.

ADJUSTING THE LENGTH OF THE STITCH REPEATS

Adjust the length of the stitch repeat in three ways:

Stitch length dial. Use the stitch length dial. This method expands the space between the stitches. If the stitch length becomes too long, the pattern resembles a shaped zigzag rather than a satin stitched shape. (See Fig. 10-1.)

Thread weights. Combine stitch

Detail of *Christmas Wreath* wallhanging; note the satin stitching in the bow, straight stitch embroidery and outlining.

Basic stitch

Shortened using fine thread and stitch length

Lengthened using double thread and stitch length

Lengthened with stitch length only

Lengthened with elongation feature on computerized machines

Fig. 10-1

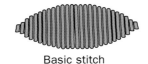

Use two half circles to make a large circle

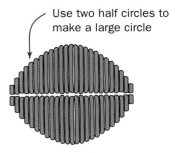

Fig. 10-2

❑ To keep the original stitch proportion and ensure true circles, adjust the stitch width and length.

❑ Use the Pattern Begin and Single Pattern feature on your machine for the best results.

❑ Usually, narrowing the stitch width requires shortening the stitch length. The circle will appear oval when the stitch length is too long for the stitch width.

❑ For the smallest circles choose size 50, 60, or 80 cotton machine embroidery thread.

🌸 **Caution**

Remember to knot the beginning and end of each pattern to prevent the stitches from pulling out.

length with differing thread weights. For a short stitch repeat, use fine thread and a short stitch length. For longer stitch repeats, use a thick thread or double threads and a longer stitch length. This method is extremely successful on older non-computerized machines.

Elongation setting. Use the elongation setting on the machine. Most computerized machines allow the user to lengthen the pattern repeat without affecting the density of the satin stitch. It lengthens the pattern by adding stitches, not expanding the space between the stitches.

MAKING SATIN STITCH CIRCLES

Stitched circles and half circles are the perfect replacement for small appliquéd circles. Use the stitches that create circles and half circles to make a wide variety of circle sizes.

❑ For large circles, join two half circles (see Fig. 10-2).

❑ For smaller circles, use the circle patterns or the daisy petal pattern.

Samples that I made to practice satin stitching in circles. I keep these as a reference in one of my three binders.

Advanced Methods: Start the pattern repeat by taking one stitch and pulling the bobbin thread through the fabric. Hold both thread tails *in front* on the presser foot. As you begin stitching, catch the thread tails under the stitches. Stitch about one half of the pattern repeat then clip the thread tails close to the stitching. This makes a neat and secure start to the pattern repeat and reduces the number of thread tails requiring knotting and clipping.

Sew A Sample

TAPERED SATIN STITCH SAMPLE

Supplies

- 10" square block of plain cotton broadcloth backed with freezer paper

Machine Setup

Widest zigzag stitch

Satin stitch length of .5 or shorter

Loosen the top tension at least one number. On the wrong side, roughly divide the width of the stitch into thirds. The center third is bobbin thread; the outer two thirds, needle thread.

MAKING A PERFECT SATIN STITCH

First, practice making a perfect satin stitch:

1 Adjust the stitch length so the stitches touch each other without overlapping or having gaps.

2 Loosen the top tension. A loosened tension prevents tunneling or puckering of the

fabric. In addition, the loosened top tension makes a smooth stitch edge by pulling the top thread to the back of the stitch. That keeps the bobbin thread, and the knots formed by the interlocking of the bobbin and needle threads, on the back of the block, not on the stitch edges.

TAPERING THE SATIN STITCH

Tapering is a basic satin stitch skill. Made by varying the stitch width during stitching, tapering requires a steady hand (see Fig. 10-3). The trick is to make a smooth, well-shaped taper that fits the shape of the appliqué pieces. Tapering is

Tapered satin stitches create veins in the leaves of this *Floral Urns* quilt block.

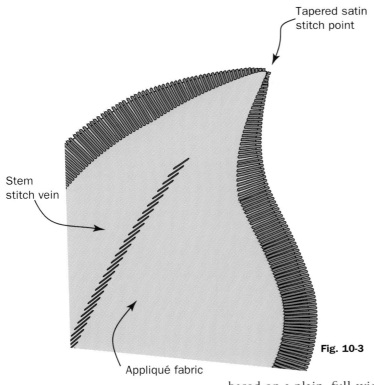

Tapered satin stitch point

Stem stitch vein

Appliqué fabric

Fig. 10-3

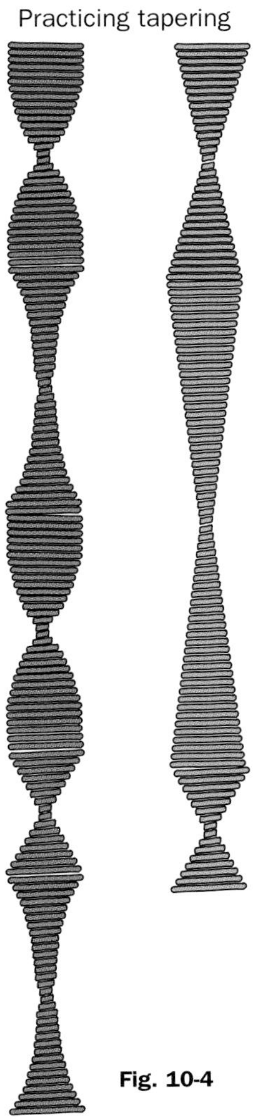

Practicing tapering

Fig. 10-4

Notice that the speed with which you adjust the width affects the appearance of the taper. Tapers can be long and narrow or short and wide. They can have straight, concave, or convex edges (see Fig. 10-5). Make two or three rows of stitching, practicing your tapering skills.

Don't look at the stitch width control. Keep your focus on the line of stitching. By watching the stitching line, you can readily adjust the size and shape of the taper.

Machine Savvy

WHAT IF MY TAPERING ISN'T SATISFACTORY?

If you are unhappy with your basic tapering, refer to your sewing machine's owner's manual. Many machines have built-in tapers that automatically make smooth, well-shaped tapers at a touch of a button. Note that your taper samples might not look like those in Figures 10-4 and 10-5. Machines taper in different ways. Some machines move smoothly between the stitch widths, others have block tapers that look like stair steps.

based on a plain, full-width satin stitch and doesn't require a built-in pattern.

When you are ready to practice tapering the satin stitch, begin stitching at one end of the fabric block. Stitch across the block. As you stitch, adjust the stitch width a number of times—wide to narrow and back to wide (see Fig. 10-4).

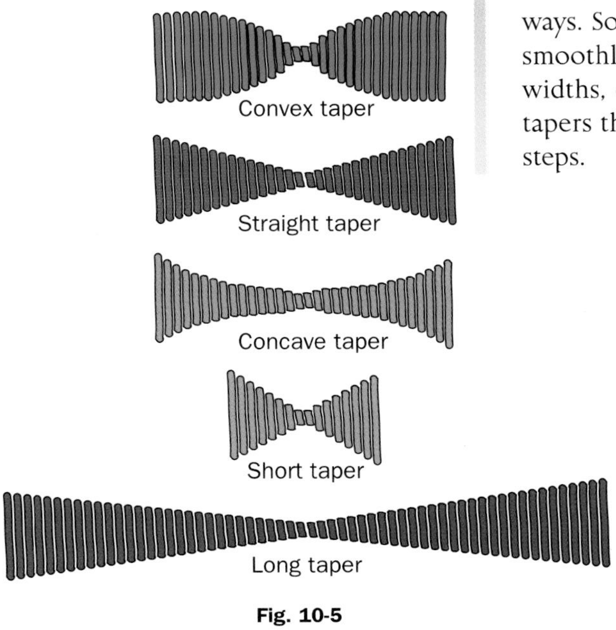

Convex taper

Straight taper

Concave taper

Short taper

Long taper

Fig. 10-5

CUSTOMIZING THE SATIN STITCH

The samples in the previous section used the full stitch width. The stitch width varied from the widest to the narrowest (a straight stitch) and back to the widest. This set-up is the easiest, but is not suitable for every application. A full width zigzag obscures small leaves or stems. On small scale designs the maximum stitch width should be less than full width, perhaps 1.5 or 2.0. This causes problems when the stitch width control doesn't have stops or guides to tell you when you have reached the desired stitch width. It places you in the unenviable position of trying to make a smooth taper and at the same time watching the stitch width control.

There are a number of ways to solve the problem, depending on the features of the machine's stitch width control.

❑　With a push button stitch width control, the easiest way to solve this problem is by counting the number of times you press the button. This will give you an accurate width.

❑　Some machines employ a system of clicks or stops. The stitch width control may have stops you can feel when slowly turning the dial. Simply count the stops to know the width.

❑　On some machines, the Double Needle feature affects maximum stitch width. Engaging the Double Needle feature guarantees the maximum stitch width setting. The machine can taper at any width below the maximum setting, but cannot go wider. On the Viking #1, the Double Needle feature reduces the stitch width to 3.0. On the Bernina 1530, the double needle feature gives you three

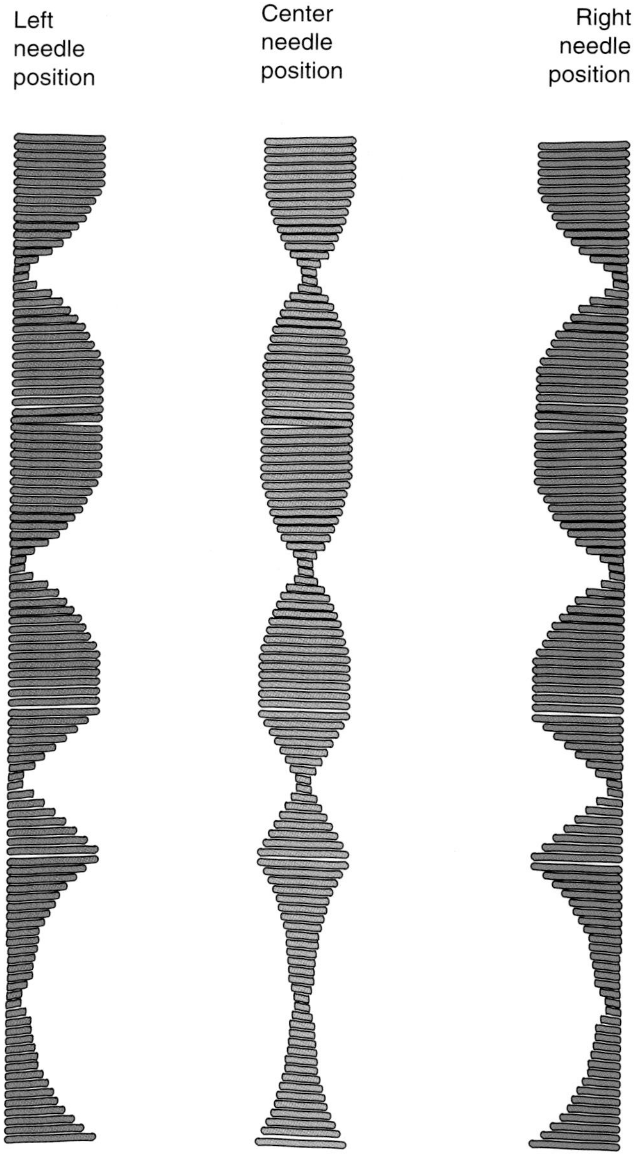

Left needle position

Center needle position

Right needle position

Fig. 10-6

choices. The first choice sets the maximum width at slightly over 3.0, the second choice sets the maximum width at 2.25, and the last choice sets the maximum width at 1.5.

TAPERING TRICKS

The following are a few of my tapering tricks:

1　On leaves or stems, start at the narrowest end of the pattern. The point is the most visible and important part of the pattern. Starting with the point will ensure a smooth taper even if you don't reach the widest stitch width before reaching the edge of the appliqué piece.

2　Always sew three or four straight stitches at the point of the taper. This ensures a sharp point and a secure knot.

3 For machines with adjustable needle positions, try tapering with left or right needle positions (see Fig. 10-6). The needle position will affect the appearance of the taper. In the center needle position, the taper narrows from each edge of the stitch. In the left needle position, the taper narrows from the right edge and maintains the left edge of the stitch. The opposite happens in the right needle position. Use needle positions when the design has one straight edge and one tapered edge.

SUCCESSFULLY FITTING THE SATIN STITCH TO THE APPLIQUÉ OR DESIGN LINE

Satin stitched edges give the best results with raw edge appliqué. Satin stitched veins, stems and embroidery work well with turned edge appliqué.

Some designs are meant to be tapered at both ends of the line of stitches. Other designs include multiple tapers along the stitching line.

Satin stitch edging can be combined with invisible stitching or used alone to stitch the appliqué in place. In either application, guide the edge of the appliqué under the right stitch edge. The stitch placement on the appliqué piece is one stitch on the appliqué, one stitch off the appliqué. When stitching clockwise, the needle in the right hand swing should pierce only the background fabric, yet be as close as possible to the appliqué's edge.

Concealing the fabric edges on raw edge corners is difficult with tapering. It is important that the tapering stitch completely cover the edges of the appliqué point. I routinely stitch the corner slightly longer than the actual size of the appliqué piece. This completely encloses the fabric in stitches. To make a super sharp point, end the taper with at least three straight stitches.

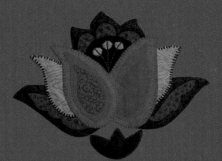

Part Four

QUILT BINDINGS

Basic bindings: The blue prairie point binding is finished with mock binding. The pink binding is plain French binding. The printed fabrics are the right sides of the quilts; the plain muslin is on the wrong side. Shown with a blind hem foot.

CHAPTER 11

Binding Basics

BEAUTY IS IN THE DETAILS: a finely crafted binding transforms a simple quilt into a masterpiece. Binding is my favorite part of quilt making. I'm always looking for new and better ways to bind using machine features, and there are dozens of innovative and breathtaking binding possibilities. Use the sewing machine's features to make binding easier, faster, and more innovative. Two methods, French binding and mock binding, are the basis for most decorative bindings. Mastery of these two methods is required in order to make successful decorative bindings.

BASIC MACHINE-STITCHED FRENCH BINDING

There are a number of ways to bind a quilt. The most durable and professional looking binding is a double-fold binding called French binding. In the traditional French binding method, the binding is first stitched to the quilt top and then hand stitched to the quilt backing. By comparison, I use a French binding method completely stitched by machine. First, stitch the binding to the quilt back, and then topstitch on the quilt front. The only hand stitching required closes the mitered corners.

Like all French bindings, this method uses bias strips cut from extra quilt fabric. Cut the strips six times the finished size of the binding, thus a $^1/_2$" finished binding is cut 3" wide.

MAKING THE BINDING

Begin with the yardage required in the pattern or use one of the many charts available to help determine the yardage requirements. Prepare all binding fabrics with medium to heavy starch (see page 20). The heavier the starch, the easier it is to bind the quilt.

Stitch the short ends of bias strips together to make a single long length of bias. Fold the bias in half, lengthwise, wrong sides together, lining up the raw edges. Press carefully. Do not stretch the bias edges.

STARTING THE BINDING

Before binding the quilt, trim the quilt to the finished size including the binding width. Start the binding in a corner to make the neatest possible join. The miter is the perfect place to conceal the seam that will join the two ends of binding. Also, placing the join in the corner allows you to use complex pipings and edgings.

1 Begin by marking the exact corner of the stitching lines on the quilt body. The seam allowance of the binding should be slightly less than the width of the finished binding. A ½" binding requires a generous ⅜" seam allowance. Measure a generous ⅜" in from each corner and mark with a pin.

2 Place the binding on the *wrong* side of the quilt. Start in the corner. The end of the binding should extend at least 2" beyond the edge of the quilt. Line up the raw edges of the binding and the quilt. Start stitching at the exact corner of the stitching lines, a generous ⅜" in from the end of the quilt edge. Backstitch to secure the corner.

3 Continue stitching along one side of the quilt.

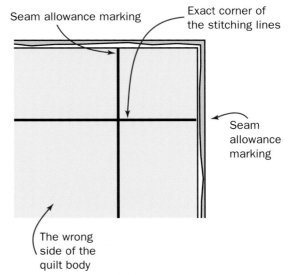

Fig. 11-1

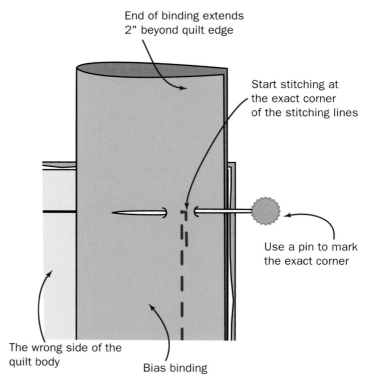

Fig. 11-2

MAKING 90° MITERED CORNERS IN FRENCH BINDING

1 To make a 90° mitered corner in a French binding, as you approach the corner measure a generous ⅜" (or the seam allowance measure) in from the next side of the quilt. Mark with a pin.

2 Sew to the pin, backstitch, and remove the quilt from the machine (see Fig. 11-3).

3 Fold the free end of the binding over the stitched binding. This will form a diagonal fold in the corner of the binding (see Fig. 11-4).

4 Hold that fold in place and fold the free end of binding back onto the quilt, lining up the binding to the quilt edge (see Fig. 11-5).

5 Resume stitching at the corner.

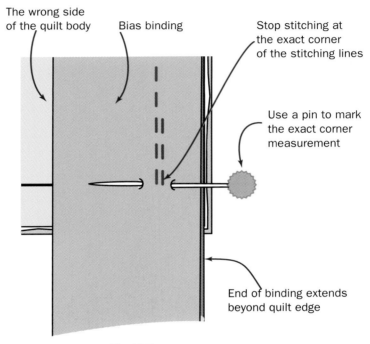

The wrong side of the quilt body

Bias binding

Stop stitching at the exact corner of the stitching lines

Use a pin to mark the exact corner measurement

End of binding extends beyond quilt edge

Fig. 11-3

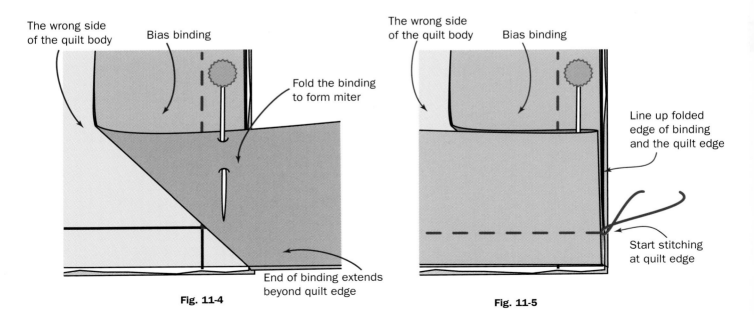

The wrong side of the quilt body

Bias binding

Fold the binding to form miter

End of binding extends beyond quilt edge

Fig. 11-4

The wrong side of the quilt body

Bias binding

Line up folded edge of binding and the quilt edge

Start stitching at quilt edge

Fig. 11-5

ENDING THE BINDING

1 Continue stitching around the quilt, making miters at each corner.

2 Upon reaching the starting corner of the quilt, fold back the beginning side of binding to prevent stitching into it. Sew to the starting stitch line to complete the beginning corner.

3 Backstitch to secure the corner.

4 Remove the quilt from the machine. Cut the end of binding to extend 2" beyond the edge of the quilt. (Note: Fig. 11-6 shows the wrong side, and Fig. 11-7 shows the same corner from the right side of the quilt body.)

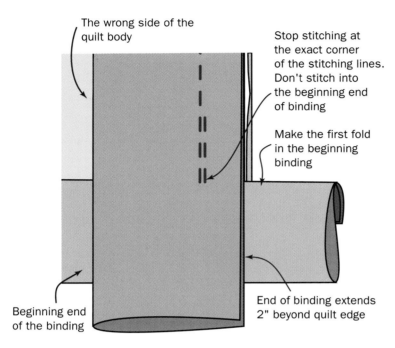

The wrong side of the quilt body

Stop stitching at the exact corner of the stitching lines. Don't stitch into the beginning end of binding

Make the first fold in the beginning binding

Beginning end of the binding

End of binding extends 2" beyond quilt edge

Fig. 11-6

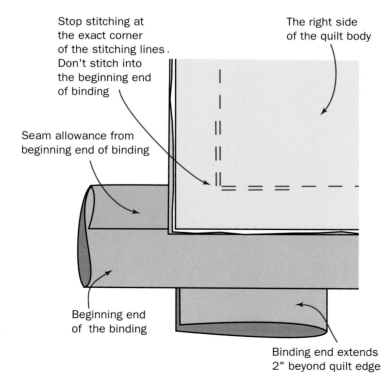

Stop stitching at the exact corner of the stitching lines. Don't stitch into the beginning end of binding

The right side of the quilt body

Seam allowance from beginning end of binding

Beginning end of the binding

Binding end extends 2" beyond quilt edge

Fig. 11-7

 Hot Tip

I suggest stabilizing the edges of a quilt before finishing the binding. Before turning the binding, set up the machine for the longest and widest zigzag. Use this stitch to overcast the raw edges of the quilt and binding. The overcast flattens the edge of the quilt and ensures an even width binding. Don't try to overcast the corners; simply skip them.

JOINING THE BINDING ENDS WITH A MITERED CORNER

This method of binding doesn't fold the binding exactly in half when it covers the raw edge. The front portion of the binding is always slightly wider than the back of the binding. To make the correct miter requires knowing the exact fold line of the binding.

1 To find the correct fold line, fold the beginning section of the binding to the quilt front. Determine the correct placement of the binding on the right side of the quilt. Press a short distance in from the corner to crease the fold line of the binding. (See Fig. 11-8.)

2 Open the binding. Fold the binding and quilt to line up all the raw edges of the corner and the binding. Pin to secure the raw edges.

3 With the creased binding on top, mark the miters. Use a ruler with a 45° mark. Place the 45° line on the fold. The first miter is from the last corner stitch to the fold. The second miter is from the fold to the finished edge.

4 Stitch the mitered corner starting at the finished edge of the binding. Make sure the finished edges line up exactly. To make a neat start, begin stitching about ¼" into the binding, reverse to the finished edge, then stitch forward to complete the miter. Stitch toward the outer point of the miter.

5 Stitch to the first stitching line. Backstitch to secure.

6 Trim the seam allowances and press open the miter seam.

 **Hot Tip**

The outer point of a miter is extremely sharp. This sharp point doesn't make an acceptable finished corner. To make a great corner, shorten the point by taking one stitch across the point rather than stitching into the exact point.

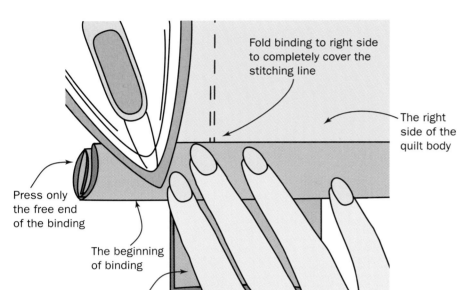

Fold binding to right side to completely cover the stitching line

The right side of the quilt body

Press only the free end of the binding

The beginning of binding

End of binding

Fig. 11-8

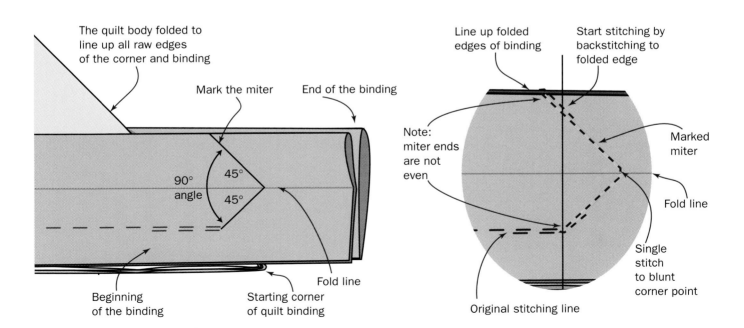

The quilt body folded to line up all raw edges of the corner and binding

Mark the miter

End of the binding

90° angle

45°

45°

Fold line

Beginning of the binding

Starting corner of quilt binding

Fig. 11-9

Line up folded edges of binding

Start stitching by backstitching to folded edge

Note: miter ends are not even

Marked miter

Fold line

Single stitch to blunt corner point

Original stitching line

Fig. 11-10

FINISHING THE BINDING

Turn the binding over the raw edges to the quilt front. Miter the front corners to match the back corners. Pin the binding in place.

Sewing Savvy

Pinning is not the only way to hold the binding in place during stitching. The following two wonderful methods work better than pins.

Use gluestick. Apply the gluestick to the quilt edge as you fold the binding over the raw edges. Hold for a few seconds, or clip with hair clips until dry.

Use a fusible thread like ThreadFuse. Fusible thread is a sewing thread that acts like fusible web when heated. Use fusible thread in the bobbin. It is slightly heavier than normal thread and requires that you use the extra bobbin case for novelty threads. Slight tension adjustments may be necessary. Use the fusible thread when making the initial line of straight stitching, or when zigzag stitching. Stitch with the right side of the quilt down, so the fusible thread is on the right side of the quilt. To activate, fold the binding over the raw edges and press with an iron on a steam setting. The fusible thread can replace the second line of stitching for wall hangings or other quilts that don't require frequent laundering.

Using an open toe embroidery foot or an edgestitch foot, stitch the binding to the quilt. The thickness of the binding can make it difficult to hold the foot on the binding. The foot slips off the binding onto the thinner quilt body. In that case, substitute a bulky fabric foot for the edgestitch foot. Guide the binding under the thinner portion of the foot. The edge of the binding rests against the slight raise formed by the thicker portion of the foot. This foot allows the extra thickness of the binding to feed smoothly, plus the raise in the foot acts as an edgestitch foot. Frequently, these feet also require variable needle positions to align the straight stitch correctly on the binding edge.

Machine Savvy

USING AN EDGESTITCH FOOT

A number of feet are suitable for edge stitching, including the edgestitch foot and blind hem foot. These feet are among many feet with a metal or plastic guide (see Fig. 11-11). The guide rides along the edge of the fabric and ensures perfectly-placed topstitching. Any foot will work that allows you to guide to the left of the finished edge and stitch on the right side of the finished edge. Frequently, these feet require variable needle positions.

Stitch $1/8$" in from the folded edge of the binding. Correctly done, the topstitching will be a straight neat line on the top of the quilt. From the wrong side of the quilt the stitching will miss the back binding by $1/16$" to $1/8$".

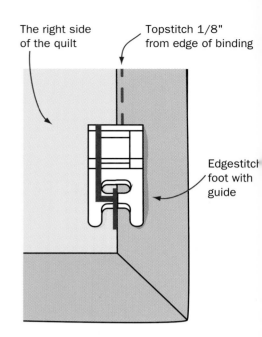

The right side of the quilt

Topstitch 1/8" from edge of binding

Edgestitch foot with guide

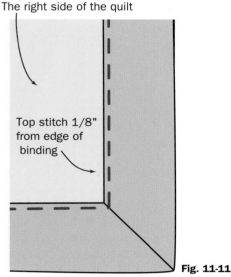

The right side of the quilt

Top stitch 1/8" from edge of binding

Fig. 11-11

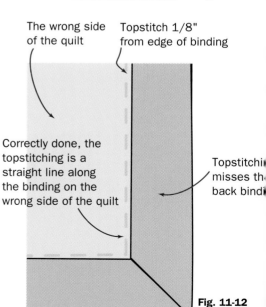

The wrong side of the quilt

Topstitch 1/8" from edge of binding

Correctly done, the topstitching is a straight line along the binding on the wrong side of the quilt

Topstitching misses the back binding

Fig. 11-12

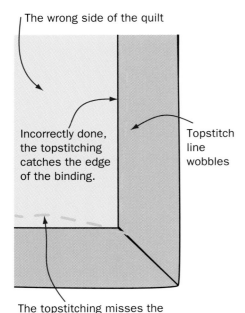

The wrong side of the quilt

Incorrectly done, the topstitching catches the edge of the binding.

Topstitch line wobbles

The topstitching misses the back binding by more than 1/8"

Fig. 11-13

If the topstitching on the front binding does not line up correctly with the binding on the quilt back, the reasons can include irregular seam allowances, not cutting the binding accurately, or not allowing for the thickness of the quilt batt.

My best advice is to make sample bindings before proceeding with the actual binding. The sample binding will show you how the finished binding will look, and even how to correct any problems before cutting the actual binding. I use a short 12" end of scrap fabrics to sample bind the actual quilt.

 **Hot Tip**

Stitch a sample binding using Wash Away Basting thread. The thread disappears when pressed with heavy steam and precludes the need for ripping out stitches to remove the sample binding from the quilt.

COMMON BINDING ERRORS

There are three common binding errors:

❑ The top binding doesn't cover the stitching from the back binding.

❑ The topstitching falls into the back binding (this looks messy, because the back and front bindings never line up perfectly).

❑ The topstitching misses the back binding by more than $1/8$".

The first two problems require similar solutions. Take a narrower seam allowance when first stitching the binding to the quilt, or cut the binding $1/8$" wider. Frequently the batting and fabrics take up a slight amount of the binding. It is important to allow for the thickness when working with heavy batting or many layers of fabric. An extra $1/8$" to $1/4$" is usually sufficient for all but the heaviest batting.

The third binding error requires other solutions. Take a wider seam allowance when first stitching the binding to the quilt, or cut the binding $1/8$" narrower. The fabric and batting are too thin to take up the binding.

Options. You can use other ways to secure the binding to the quilt. In place of the straight stitch use one of the following stitches:

Blind hem or overlock stitch: Use the blind hem or overlock stitch with invisible thread. The straight stitches fall on the quilt top and the zigzag stitch catches the binding edge (see Fig. 11-14). This requires a stitch that has the straight stitch on the left and the zigs to the right. The stitch width should be as narrow as possible and still catch the binding fabric.

Narrow zigzag: Use the narrow zigzag stitch with invisible thread.

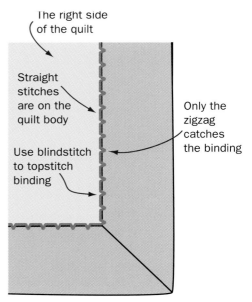

The right side of the quilt

Straight stitches are on the quilt body

Use blindstitch to topstitch binding

Only the zigzag catches the binding

Fig. 11-14

Decorative stitches: Use decorative stitches with machine embroidery thread. This includes the buttonhole stitch and feather stitching.

Fusible thread: Use fusible thread in the initial straight stitch and overcast. This thread effectively replaces the topstitching. This is best on wall hangings or infrequently washed quilts. See page 106 for more information about using fusible thread.

BASIC MACHINE-STITCHED MOCK BINDING

Making mock binding is like facing the quilt edge. Its purpose is to attach prairie points or other decorative edges without having to hand sew the quilt edges. Usually mock binding is functional, and like a garment facing, required but unseen. In this method the mock binding turns to the quilt front and becomes an important part of the quilt design.

Determine the binding width by considering the desired effect.

The binding is usually cut 1½" wide to finish ½" wide. This binding is not suitable for finished widths under ⅜" or over 1". The formula for determining the cut width is:

the finished width x 2 plus ½" (for the two ¼" seam allowances)

Cut and stitch the bias strips following the basic directions for French binding (see page 101).

STARTING THE BINDING

Before binding the quilt, trim the quilt to the finished size, including a ¼" seam allowance (see Fig. 11-1 on page 102). Start the binding in the corner to make the neatest possible join. The miter is the perfect place to conceal the seam that will join the two ends of binding. Placing the join in the corner allows the use of complex pipings and edgings (see Fig. 11-2 on page 102).

1 Begin by marking the exact corner of the stitching lines. This is ¼" in from the corners of the quilt.

2 Place the binding on the wrong side of the quilt. Start in the corner. The end of the binding should extend at least 1" beyond the edge of the quilt. Line up the raw edges of the binding and the quilt. Start stitching at the exact corner of the stitching lines ¼" in from the end of the quilt edge. Backstitch to secure the corner.

3 Continue stitching around the quilt.

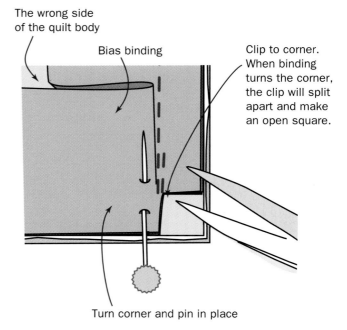

The wrong side of the quilt body

Bias binding

Clip to corner. When binding turns the corner, the clip will split apart and make an open square.

Turn corner and pin in place

Fig. 11-15

MAKING 90° MITERED CORNERS IN A BASIC MOCK BINDING

To make a 90° mitered corner in a basic mock binding, as you approach the corner, measure ¼" in from the next side of the quilt and mark with a pin. Sew to the pin, backstitch, and remove quilt from the machine.

Clip the seam allowance of the binding to the last stitch. Turn the corner with the binding, pin in place, and continue stitching the remaining edges of the quilt. The clip in the seam allowance will split at the corner, creating an open square.

ENDING THE BINDING

1 Continue stitching around the quilt, making miters at each corner.

2 Fold back the beginning side of binding to prevent stitching into it.

3 Sew to the exact corner of the quilt. Backstitch to secure the corner.

4 Remove the quilt from the machine. Cut the end of the binding to extend 1" beyond the edge of the quilt.

✿ Hot Tip

I suggest stabilizing the edge of the quilt before finishing the binding. Before turning the binding, set up the machine for the longest and widest zigzag. Use this stitch to overcast the raw edges of the quilt and binding. The overcast flattens the edge of the quilt and ensures an even width binding. Don't try to overcast the beginning corner; simply skip it.

JOINING THE BINDING ENDS WITH A MITERED CORNER

1 Fold the binding and quilt to line up all the raw edges of the corner and the binding. Pin to secure the raw edges.

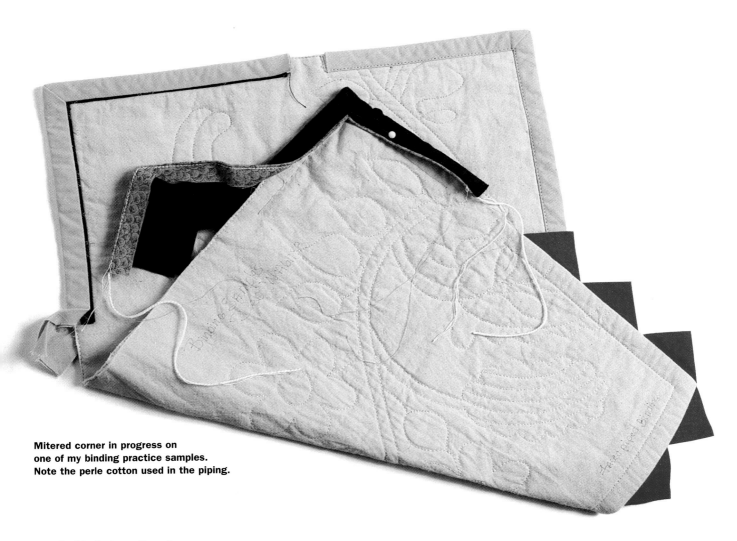

Mitered corner in progress on
one of my binding practice samples.
Note the perle cotton used in the piping.

2 Mark the mitered corner using a ruler with a 45° mark. Place the 45° line on the original stitching line. The miter extends from the finished edge to the corner. (See Fig. 11-16.)

 Hot Tip

Rather than mark a miter, simply sew along the folded edge of the quilt that is between the two layers of binding. A zipper foot makes this seam easy to stitch.

3 Stitch the mitered corner, starting at the finished edge of the binding. Stitch to first stitching line. Make sure the finished edges are exactly in

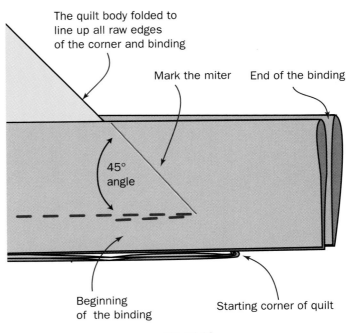

The quilt body folded to line up all raw edges of the corner and binding

Mark the miter End of the binding

45° angle

Beginning of the binding

Starting corner of quilt

Fig. 11-16

line. To make a neat start, begin stitching about ¼" into the binding, then reverse to the finished edge, and stitch forward to complete the miter. Trim the seam allowances and press open the miter seam.

4 Miter the remaining corners by stitching, trimming, and pressing following the basic directions for the mitered join.

FINISHING THE BINDING

To finish the binding, trim away the seam allowances at the corners of the quilt. Tip the binding to the right side of the quilt and press. Secure the binding with pins. To help shape the corner, use a point turner, making the corner square. The corner points of this binding are always slightly rounded because of the thickness of the layers at the point of the corner.

 Hot Tip

Pinning is not the only way to hold the binding in place during stitching. Use a gluestick. Apply the glue to the quilt edge as you fold the binding over the raw edges. Hold for a few seconds, or clip with hair clips, until dry.

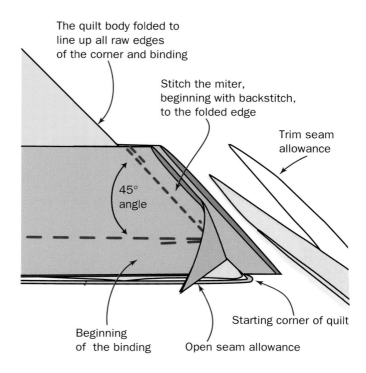

The quilt body folded to line up all raw edges of the corner and binding

Stitch the miter, beginning with backstitch, to the folded edge

Trim seam allowance

45° angle

Beginning of the binding

Open seam allowance

Starting corner of quilt

Fig. 11-17

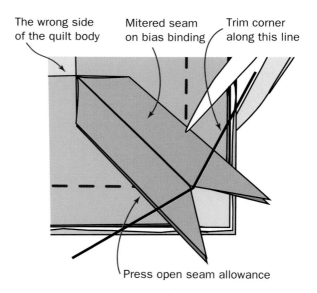

The wrong side of the quilt body

Mitered seam on bias binding

Trim corner along this line

Press open seam allowance

Fig. 11-18

Topstitch the binding to the right side of the quilt using an open toe embroidery foot or edge stitch foot. Stitch $\frac{1}{8}$" in from the folded edge of the binding.

 **Sewing Savvy**

What should you do when the corners don't turn out square? Mock binding has a tendency to become "dog-eared" at the corners. Dog-eared corners finish at less than 90°, even though the corners were true 90° angles prior to binding. To compensate for the effect and prevent dog-ears, widen the angle of the corners by trimming the quilt corners prior to binding (see Fig. 11-20). Remove a small wedge of fabric from each side of the corners. The wedge measures $1\frac{1}{2}$" long, starting at $\frac{1}{8}$" in from the corner and extending off the quilt at the $1\frac{1}{2}$" mark.

Options. You can use other stitches to topstitch the binding to the quilt:

Blind hem or overlock stitch: Use the blind hem or overlock stitch with invisible thread. The straight stitches fall on the quilt top and the zigzag stitch catches the binding edge. This requires a stitch that has the straight stitch on the left and zigs to the right. The stitch width should be as narrow as possible and still catch the binding fabric.

Zigzag stitch: Use a narrow zigzag stitch with invisible thread.

Decorative stitches: Use decorative stitches with machine embroidery thread. This includes the buttonhole stitch and feather stitch.

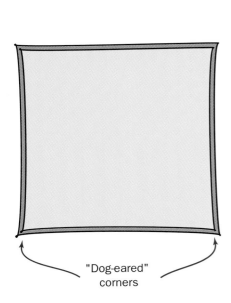

"Dog-eared" corners

Fig. 11-19

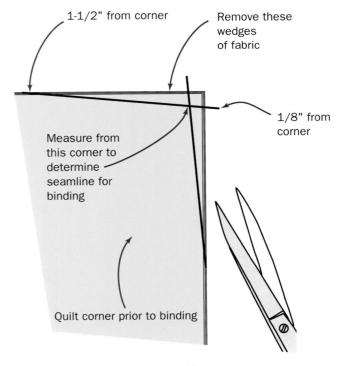

1-1/2" from corner

Remove these wedges of fabric

Measure from this corner to determine seamline for binding

1/8" from corner

Quilt corner prior to binding

Fig. 11-20

Three of the simplest piped bindings, from right to left: triple piping, single piping, and double piping. Shown with a pintuck foot.

Chapter 12
Piped Bindings

I ADORE PIPED BINDINGS. They are extremely versatile and give spectacular results. In its basic form, piped binding is joined to the quilt with a $1/8$" mini piping. Options can include French and mock bindings (see Chapter 11, page 101). The bindings can be piped with single, double, triple, rickrack, or shell piping. Any straight edged fine trim can be substituted for the basic piping, such as silk ribbon, metallic braids, even lace. The choices are limited only by your imagination.

There are a number of ways to use piping when binding. Traditionally, piping is stitched to the quilt prior to binding. I prefer to stitch the piping to the binding before stitching the binding to the quilt. This way every step of the binding can be machine-stitched.

 Sew A Sample

Piping Sample

Supplies
- scrap fabrics
- perle cotton or any lightweight cord
- thread

Machine Setup

Setup depends on the foot you are using to make piping; see following directions.

MAKING THE PIPING

The piping used on piped binding is the same as the mini piping used for fine stems in turned-edge appliqué. I am repeating here the basic directions for making mini piping.

1 For all mini piping cut a strip of lightly starched fabric at least 1" wide. For wider piping cut the strip 1" wider than the finished width of the piping. Make each strip as long as possible; short strips are difficult to turn evenly.

2 Make the piping by folding a strip of fabric over a cord. The secret to good piping is stitching the fabric firmly around the cord without stitching into the cord. To help achieve this effect, guide the cord into a groove on the bottom of a pintuck presser foot. The groove holds the fabric taut to the cord and prevents the cord from slipping under the needle and being caught in the stitching line.

At this point in the process, the type of foot you use determines the next steps. For these directions I'm using a seven-groove pintuck foot. Pintuck feet, including three-groove, five-groove, seven-groove, and nine-groove feet, make the best mini piping. The grooves are deep and the foot sits firmly on the feed dogs. With the machine correctly set up, it is almost impossible to stitch into the cord when using these feet. However, pintuck feet have centered grooves. With the cord in the center groove and the needle in center position, the needle will stitch into the cord. The key to successfully using this foot is to adjust the needle position to stitch directly beside the cord, not through it. Thus these feet work best with variable needle positions, especially those machines with seven or more needle positions.

3 Fold the piping fabric, right side out, around the cord. For my example I used size 3 perle cotton. The cord should extend 1" beyond the edge of the fabric. Slip the cord and fabric under the presser foot.

4 Place the cord in the selected groove of the foot, holding the seam allowances toward the right. Using a straight stitch, sew along the cord to make the piping.

PIPING HINTS

A few steps that make it easier to stitch the piping:

1 To have the fabric firmly stitched around the cord, before sewing, smooth the cord against the center fold of the fabric by rubbing the piping between the thumb and index finger of your left hand.

2 After smoothing the piping with your left hand, lay the piping against the bed of the machine.

3 Force the cord against the fold of the fabric, using your right-hand fingernails. Hold the piping firmly against the bed of the machine directly in front of the presser foot.

4 Insert into the selected groove and sew.

5 Upon completion, remove the piping from the machine. Trim the seam allowance to ¼".

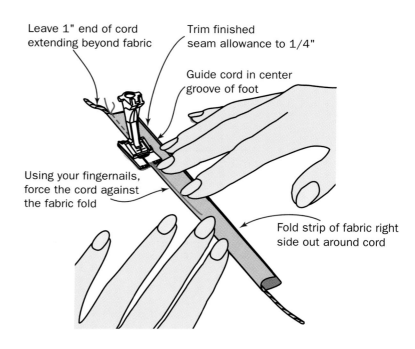

Leave 1" end of cord extending beyond fabric

Trim finished seam allowance to 1/4"

Guide cord in center groove of foot

Using your fingernails, force the cord against the fabric fold

Fold strip of fabric right side out around cord

Fig. 12-1

STITCHING THE MINI PIPING TO THE BINDING

Stitch the piping along the center of the binding before stitching the binding to the quilt. The machine settings are identical to the machine setting for making the mini piping (see page 113). *Do not alter presser foot or needle position from the original piping directions.*

1 Determine the center of the binding by measuring half the width of the binding. In my example, the binding measures 3". Half of 3" is 1½".

2 Measure this half-width amount (1½" in my example) to the right of the *needle*.

The needle position doesn't affect this measure; simply measure from the needle to the right. To guide an accurate large (e.g., 1½") seam allowance requires a seam guide or gauge. Use a short strip of vinyl tape to mark the seam guide at the half-width measurement. Place the tape to the right of the needle and foot and press it to the machine bed. Use the edge of the tape as the guide, or make a mark on the tape with a permanent fine line marker.

3 Place the binding and piping under the foot. The binding seam allowance can be to the left or right. Line up the piping in the groove in the presser foot used to stitch the original mini piping. Line up the binding edge with the half-width mark on the machine bed.

 Caution

On multiple piping or single sided trims, be sure to place the *right* side of the piping against the *right* side of the binding.

4 Lower the presser foot and stitch the piping to the binding.

 Sewing Savvy

There are two important tips to stitching the piping to the binding.

❏ Don't pull on the piping. Pulling the piping causes the feed dogs to gather the binding as it is stitched to the piping. The finished binding will not lay flat.

❏ Trust the foot to guide the piping. Don't look at the piping as you stitch. Watch the binding edge to ensure an accurate half-width (e.g., 1½") seam allowance.

5 After stitching the piping to the binding, press the binding in half along the stitching line.

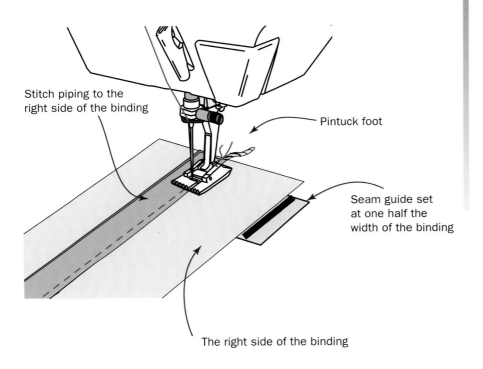

Stitch piping to the right side of the binding

Pintuck foot

Seam guide set at one half the width of the binding

The right side of the binding

Fig. 12-2

HOW TO BIND USING PIPED BINDINGS

Note that joining the binding ends at the mitered corners doesn't distort the piping or require any extra stitching to finish the piping ends. Joining the binding in the corners is the fastest and most accurate way to work with all piped bindings.

1 Follow the basic instructions for French and mock bindings on page 101. (See Fig. 12-3 and 12-4.)

2 The final line of stitching, joining front binding to the quilt, is a topstitch that falls in the seam well between the piping and binding edge. It is important to accurately straight stitch in the ditch or well of the seam to conceal the top stitching. (See Fig. 12-5.)

3 Use an open toe embroidery foot or an edge stitching foot to stitch the binding to the quilt. A number of feet can be used for edge stitching, including the edgestitch foot and blind hem foot. These feet are some of many feet with a metal or plastic guide.

The guide rides along the edge of the fabric and ensures perfectly placed top-stitching. Any foot will work that allows you to guide and stitch in the ditch or well of the seam. Frequently these feet require variable needle positions.

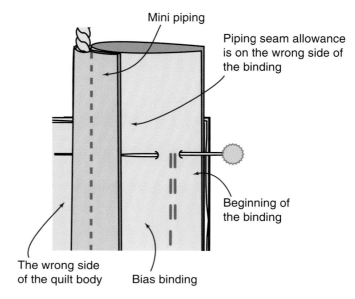

Mini piping

Piping seam allowance is on the wrong side of the binding

The wrong side of the quilt body

Bias binding

Beginning of the binding

Fig. 12-3

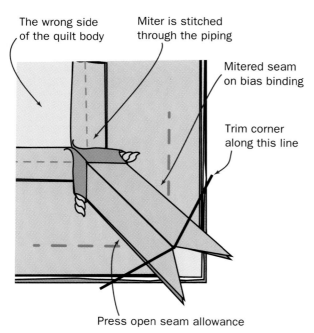

The wrong side of the quilt body

Miter is stitched through the piping

Mitered seam on bias binding

Trim corner along this line

Press open seam allowance

Fig. 12-4

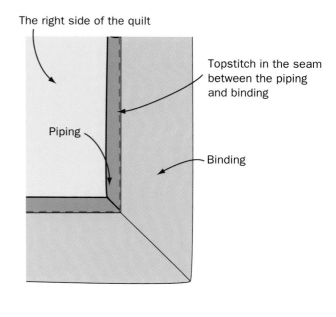

The right side of the quilt

Topstitch in the seam between the piping and binding

Piping

Binding

Fig. 12-5

DOUBLE PIPED BINDING

Double piped binding (called Beehive Binding by Elly Sienkiewicz on page 77 of her book *Design a Baltimore Album Quilt*) is made using two pipings. Traditionally, this binding is done by hand and is almost impossible to corner successfully. I substituted machine-made piping and French binding as a simple and fast alternative to the "real" thing. The results are breathtaking.

The pipings are made individually and then stitched together prior to stitching them to the quilt. This requires a presser foot with two grooves, and a sewing machine with adjustable needle positions.

 **Caution**

Multiple layer pipings have a right and wrong side. When you join two pipings, only one side shows both piping colors. The other side shows only the outer piping color. This causes some problems when stitching the piping to the binding.

There is one trick to making multiple-piped bindings. The right side of the multiple piping should be guided *up* to fit the grooves of the foot, then the two lines of piping will fit neatly into the grooves and guide easily. But the piping must be stitched right side to the binding to finish correctly. Guiding the piping and binding by following the basic instructions given earlier, where you put piping on top and binding on the bottom, will result in the wrong side of the piping facing outward on the finished quilt.

STITCHING THE MULTIPLE BINDING

To correctly stitch the multiple piping, invert the fabric layers.

1 Place the binding strip on *top* of the right side of the piping.

2 Line up the piping with the correct grooves in the presser foot, and line up the binding edge with the half-width (1½") mark on the machine bed.

3 Lower the presser foot and stitch. It may be difficult to see and guide the piping under binding fabric. However, with most binding fabrics the fabric molds to the piping and will guide in the grooves of the foot without much assistance. Stiff or thick binding fabric can be more difficult to use. If you're having trouble, there are other methods for this step. For example, I recommend using a zipper foot and following the basic instructions on page 36. For more help on doing this see the advanced method options on page 38.

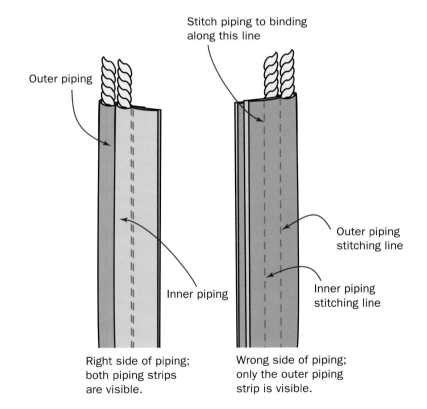

Stitch piping to binding along this line

Outer piping

Inner piping

Outer piping stitching line

Inner piping stitching line

Right side of piping; both piping strips are visible.

Wrong side of piping; only the outer piping strip is visible.

Fig. 12-6

TRIPLE-PIPED BINDINGS

Triple-piped binding uses three lines of piping. It is stitched using the double-piped binding directions. This method is best with super-fine piping and lightweight fabrics.

RICKRACK PIPED BINDINGS

Rickrack piped binding is a personal favorite. It uses baby or mini rickrack as a piping. The result is a line of tiny points that resemble tiny prairie points. The effect is charming and *so* easy. The presser feet do all the work; even a child could stitch this piped binding.

I recommend you use the Sequins'N Ribbon foot. The plastic $1/4$" guide holds the rickrack flat

Sample of first step in adding rickrack piping; first you attach rickrack to fold of binding.

Three unique pipings, from right to left: rickrack piping, uncorded piping, and shell piping.

and straight as it is stitched in place. Directions accompany the foot, but operating the foot is so simple, instructions are almost unnecessary.

You can stitch rickrack without the Sequins'N Ribbon foot by using the regular embroidery foot. The method is a little more involved but gives the same results:

1 Use the regular embroidery foot. This foot has a large groove on the sole of the foot with a regular bridge and needle hole opening.

2 Place the end of the rickrack into the needle hole opening of the foot. Thread it from the top, through the hole, and under the foot so that the rickrack lies on top of the bridge of the foot and under the sole of the foot. Let a 1" end of rickrack extend beyond the presser foot.

3 Place the binding strip under the presser foot and rickrack. Stitch in the center of the strip, lightly holding the rickrack above the bridge of the foot. Stitch slowly. The rickrack will bounce in the needle hole opening of the foot, but will feed evenly as it is stitched.

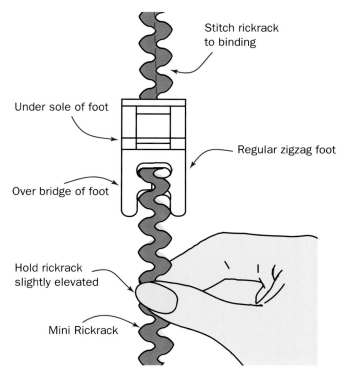

Stitch rickrack to binding

Under sole of foot

Regular zigzag foot

Over bridge of foot

Hold rickrack slightly elevated

Mini Rickrack

Fig. 12-7

 ## Caution

Don't pull on the rickrack; rather, pull gently on the binding strip. Don't expect the points of the rickrack to miter perfectly on the binding corners.

SHELL PIPED BINDINGS

Shell piped binding uses a shell edging made with a soft fabric strip and the machine's blind hem stitch. The effect is a blend between regular piping and rickrack piping. Soft curves of color extend beyond the binding edge. The blind hem stitch used for this effect is made of a combination of straight stitches and a single zigzag stitch.

 ## Sew A Sample

SHELL PIPED BINDING SAMPLE

Supplies

• Shell fabric: soft, unstarched fabrics like silks or silk-like fabrics, cotton batiste, or voile

• Binding scrap from a previous sample

Machine Setup

Blindhem stitch

Widest possible stitch width

Medium stitch length (the stitch length is determined by the desired results—short stitch length makes small shells; long stitch length makes larger shells.)

MAKING SHELLS

1 Cut a 1" bias strip from shell fabric and seam as per basic piping instructions (see page 36). Fold the strip in half and press lightly.

2 Guide the folded edge of the shell fabric along the inside left toe of the presser foot when the blindhem stitch zigzags to the left. Reverse the fold direction if the stitch zigzags to the right. On the zigzag stitch the needle

should just clear the fold of the fabric and be stitching in "air." The zigzag stitch will pull in the folded edge of the fabric, forming a shell. Slightly tighten the top tension to increase the effect.

ATTACHING PIPING TO BINDING

To attach the piping to the binding:

1 Fold and press the binding strip in half to find the strip center.

2 Using gluestick, glue the piping in place along the fold. Line up the straight stitch line with the fold of the binding strip.

3 After the glue has dried,

unfold the binding and stitch the piping to the binding.

Advanced Methods: I have suggested two ways to stitch the piping to the middle of the binding strip. One way uses tape on the bed of the machine as a seam guide. The second method uses gluestick to glue the piping in place along the center fold of the binding. There is yet another way to center piping strips on the binding strips. You can *guess* at the placement. It sounds inaccurate, but it is reliable. It is a good method when using flat trims like lace for piping.

1 Begin by cutting the binding strip ½" wider than is required. (The excess is cut away after stitching the piping.)

2 Press the center fold in the binding strip. Open the binding strip and use the fold line as a guide to place the piping. Don't worry about small deviations from the line.

3 After stitching the piping to the binding, refold and press the binding along the piping.

4 Using a rotary ruler, mat and cutter, trim the binding to the correct width. Trimming compensates for any guiding errors.

MORE PIPING IDEAS

Single uncorded piping is a traditional piping choice. Make the piping using an edgestitch foot.

1 Fold and press a narrow strip of fabric wrong sides together, or substitute a single, unfolded layer of silk ribbon for the folded fabric strips.

2 Guide the folded edge of the strip along the guide of the edgestitch foot.

3 Adjust the foot or needle position to stitch a ⅛" or ¹⁄₁₆" piping. With care, you can make the piping and stitch it to the binding simultaneously.

🪡 Sewing Savvy

When using silk ribbons or flat trims for uncorded piping, use the Sequins 'N Ribbon foot to guide and stitch the trim in place. The Sequins 'N Ribbon foot has adapters for ¹/₈", ¹/₄", and ¹/₂" widths.

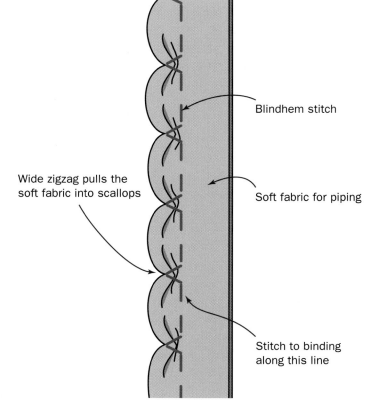

Wide zigzag pulls the soft fabric into scallops

Blindhem stitch

Soft fabric for piping

Stitch to binding along this line

Fig. 12-8

Chapter 13
Scallop Edge Binding

I AM INTRIGUED with the gorgeous scallop edge binding on the Updegraf Baltimore Album quilt (circa 1850). I first saw it in Elly Sienkiewicz's 1991 book, *Baltimore Beauties and Beyond*. Then in her 1992 book, *Design a Baltimore Album Quilt*, Elly gave basic instructions for this unique binding. One small problem: I love the binding but hate the handwork involved in duplicating the antique binding. I made changes in the basic binding to make it entirely machine-stitched. I chose to combine the scallop edge with a mock binding. The scallop edging is stitched first, then attached to the quilt with the mock binding, much like attaching a row of prairie points. Speed and simplicity of stitching compensate for the lack in authenticity. Even modified, the binding retains its beauty and elegance.

There are two major concerns with this binding: finding an easy method to stitch a repeating scallop, and fitting the scallop to the quilt edge to form pleasing and balanced corners. Because of the multitude of options in dealing with these concerns, I explain the options and their advantages and disadvantages before providing step-by-step directions.

BASIC DIRECTIONS FOR CUTTING THE STRIPS FOR THE SCALLOP

1. Heavily starch the fabric prior to cutting the strips.

2. Determine the width of the strip by the depth of the scallop. The basic strip should measure twice the depth of the scallop plus 2". This allows for seam allowances and for trimming the strip. The specific directions for each option will give information about how to measure and cut the strips for each technique.

3. The strips can be straight or bias cut. Join the strips into single strips long enough for the quilt edges.

4 Fold the strip in half, right sides together. For easier handling, press a strip of freezer paper to one side of the fabric strip.

5 The scallop edging is a very lightweight finish for the quilt. I suggest using a third layer of fabric to act as interfacing. This gives the scallop weight and body. Interfaced scallops hang better and last longer. The interfacing is cut one half the cut width of the scal-lop strip. For the interfacing layer choose another strip of scallop fabric or plain muslin. Other interfacing choices include medium-weight sew-in interfacing or lightweight needle-punch batting. I used polyester felt in the samples. Pin or glue the interfacing layer to the fabric strip. Sew with the interfacing on the bottom.

Scallop Option #1: Using a Circle Maker to Make a Simple Scallop

Sew A Sample

Circle Maker Scallop Sample

Supplies

- Circle maker or thumbtack
- Fabric strips 5" wide
- Freezer paper

Machine Setup

Average stitch length

Open toe presser foot

Basic scallop bindings showing corner alternatives, clockwise from lower left: A two color scallop binding made by offsetting two layers of scallop edgings (the underlayer has a full mitered corner, the upper layer an open corner); a single layer, full mitered corner set with piped mock binding; an open corner set with rickrack-piped mock binding; and a partial corner set with mock binding, topstitched using the blind hem stitch. Shown with a circle maker.

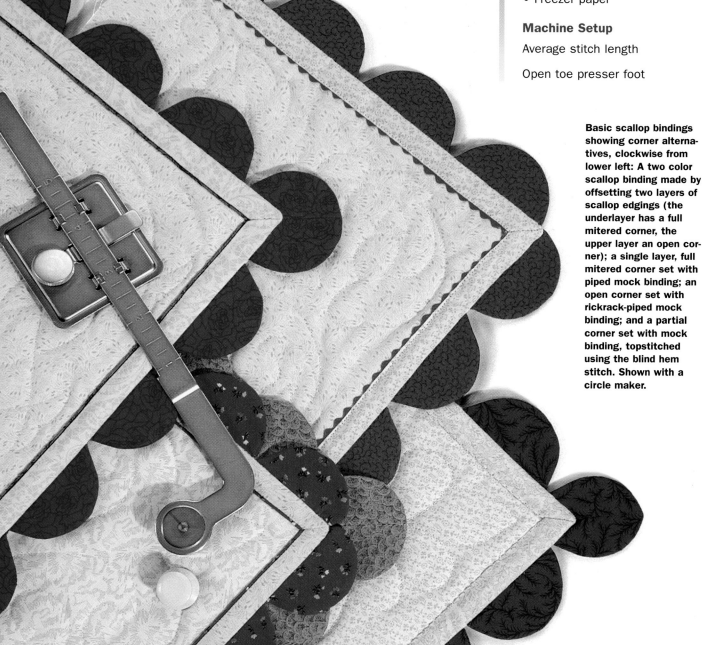

My favorite methods for making scallops use the circle maker. The simple scallop in option #1 is the easiest and best method to make scallop edging. It makes perfect mitered corners and the method works on any machine. It requires a circle maker or you can use the thumbtack method of circle making. For more directions on using circle makers see page 71.

The beauty of this binding depends on a row of evenly spaced and stitched scallops. The scallop edging includes the curved scallop and a short spacer between each scallop. The spacer makes it easier to clip and turn the scallop edge.

The strip measures twice the depth of the scallop plus 2". Follow directions on page 121 to cut the strips, then take these steps:

1 Using a fabric marker, mark a ½" seam allowance along the cut edge of the fabric strip. This is the base or guideline for the scallops. The base of the scallops rests on this line.

2 Place the circle maker on the sewing machine and adjust it for the radius of the desired circle size. For this example I'm locating the thumbtack ¾" to the left of the needle, to make a 1½" scallop.

3 Beginning on the right end of the strip, hold the strip with the folded edge to the front and the raw edges to the back (see Fig. 13-2). Place the guideline over the tack point or circle maker. Turn the strip to place the guideline directly under the needle. Keeping the interfacing on the bottom, press the fabric onto the point. Place your index and middle finger on either side of the point. When stitching, gently rotate your hand with the fabric to help pivot the fabric smoothly around the point.

 Hot Tip

Use the walking foot to evenly feed fabric layers when stitching half circles.

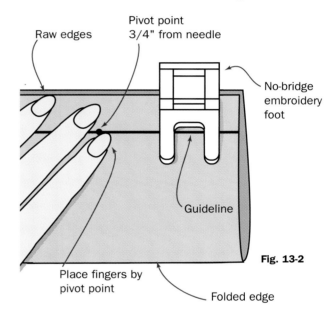

Raw edges

Pivot point 3/4" from needle

No-bridge embroidery foot

Guideline

Place fingers by pivot point

Folded edge

Fig. 13-2

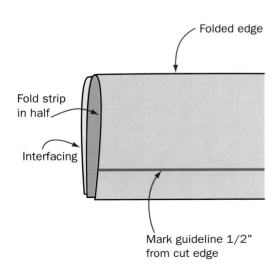

Folded edge

Fold strip in half

Interfacing

Mark guideline 1/2" from cut edge

Fig. 13-1

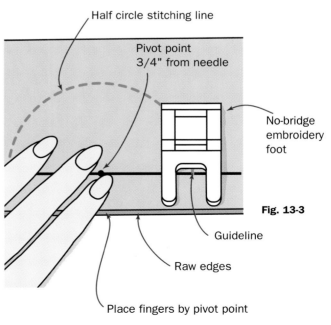

Half circle stitching line

Pivot point 3/4" from needle

No-bridge embroidery foot

Guideline

Raw edges

Place fingers by pivot point

Fig. 13-3

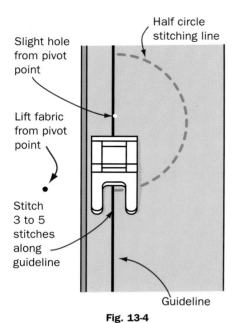

Fig. 13-4

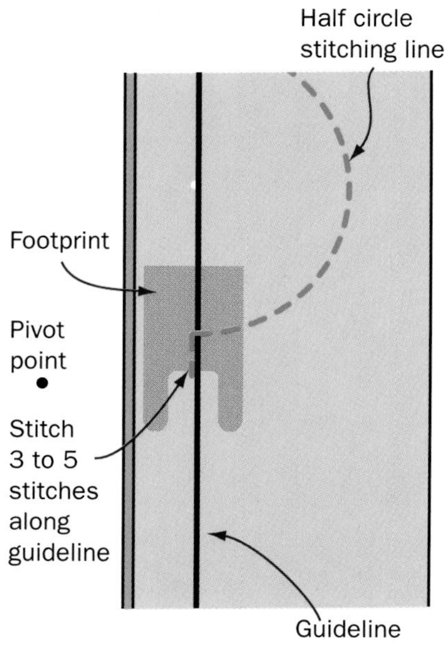

Slight hole from pivot point

Half circle stitching line

Lift fabric from pivot point

Stitch 3 to 5 stitches along guideline

Guideline

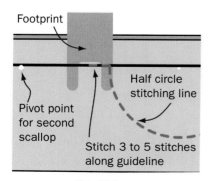

Half circle stitching line

Footprint

Pivot point

Stitch 3 to 5 stitches along guideline

Guideline

Fig. 13-5

Footprint

Half circle stitching line

Pivot point for second scallop

Stitch 3 to 5 stitches along guideline

Fig. 13-6

4 Stitch a half circle, from line to line. Stop with the needle lowered in the line. Lift the presser foot and slip the fabric off the point of the thumbtack.

5 Pivot the fabric strip and take three to five stitches along the guideline. The straight stitch spacer should measure about ¼". This spacer provides room for clipping and turning the finished scallop. The finished measurement of each scallop repeat is the diameter of the circle plus the ¼" for the straight stitch spacer.

6 Stop with the needle lowered in the line. Lift the presser foot and pivot the fabric to place the line over the point of the tack or circle maker.

Continue stitching the half circles and straight stitch spacers.

7 Trim and clip the corners and curves. Turn the strip right side out and press with steam. Use pinking shears to trim around the scallop. The inner clip of the pinker should be next to the line of stitching without cutting it. Use regular scissors or shears to clip the inside corners. Use the rounded end of a metal fingernail file to turn the curved edges.

8 After completing the scallops, trim the straight edge seam allowance to ¼". When stitched to the quilt, the base of the scallop is in the binding seam.

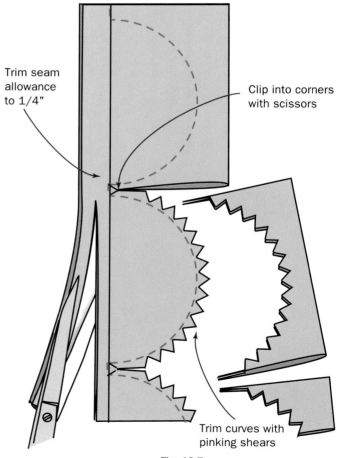

Trim seam allowance to 1/4"

Clip into corners with scissors

Trim curves with pinking shears

Fig. 13-7

GENERAL INSTRUCTIONS FOR STITCHING THE SCALLOP EDGE TO THE QUILT

To help you understand how to fit the scallop to the quilt edge, it is important that you know the basics of using the scallop edging. The wonderful part of this method is how the scallop is stitched to the quilt. Look at Figure 13-8. Prior to binding, the scallop is sewn to the wrong side of the quilt along the guideline. The seam allowance of the scallop matches the seam allowance on the quilt and binding and falls inside the finished mock binding. If you take a slightly wider seam allowance, it includes the straight stitch spacer in the scallops. This is the real key to success. The scallops can be clipped apart to help fit them to the quilt edge, and the raw edges will be completely enclosed in the seam. Clipped scallops are like prairie points and offer many design possibilities:

❏ The scallop edging can be doubled by layering two scallop edgings of different colors.

❏ Alter the space between the scallops by cutting the scallop strips into single scallops. Treat the single scallops like prairie points. The scallops can be overlapped or spaced apart. The raw edges will be covered with the binding.

❏ For a two-color scallop edging, cut two different colored scallop strips into single scallops. Alternate the colored scallops, butting the edges together.

❏ Alternate the sizes of the scallops by cutting two different sizes of scallops into single scallops. Alternate two different sizes of scallops in the same color or in two different colors.

❏ The scallop edging is not limited to being outside the binding. The scallops can be facing inward, or even stitched into a seam. The scallops can be stitched down with an appliqué stitch or left loose.

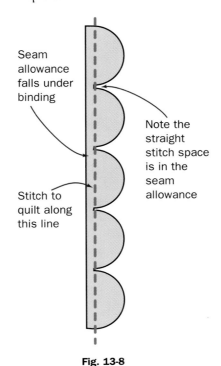

Seam allowance falls under binding

Note the straight stitch space is in the seam allowance

Stitch to quilt along this line

Fig. 13-8

FITTING THE SCALLOPS TO THE QUILT EDGE

This step has a parallel in fitting a decorative pattern to an appliqué piece. Both techniques require practice and a little luck. To fit the scallop to the quilt requires two measurements: the scallop size or repeat, and the length of the quilt side.

How the scallops fit the quilt depends on the corner style. There are two possible corner styles, the mitered corner and the open corner. The open corner is suitable for any scallop edging method, but lacks the style of the full corner.

The mitered corner is more difficult, but it is the most impressive-looking.

 **Hot Tip**

Antique quilts use the scallop edging on only three edges of the quilt. The top edge always ends on the dip of a scallop. The top edge of the quilt is bound with regular binding. Three sides require only two corners, and the method makes a longer lasting edge on the top edge of the quilt.

BASIC MEASUREMENTS FOR FITTING THE SCALLOPS

1 Determine the repeat measure of each scallop by drawing a paper pattern of the scallop and straight stitch spacer. The measure of each scallop repeat is the diameter of the circle plus the measure of the straight stitch spacer.

 **Sewing Savvy**

On thick or stiff fabrics the stitched scallop may vary in size from the original paper pattern. Before making the scallop edging, I make a fabric sample of three to five scallops to obtain an accurate measurement of the scallop repeat. For the most accurate measurement, measure the finished scallop.

2 Measure the quilt edges and estimate the approximate finished size of the quilt. The estimate is the size at which you would like the quilt to finish. The actual finished size of the quilt will be determined in the next steps. Do not trim or cut the quilt edge at this step. Frequently the estimated finished size is not the actual finished size. For example, when you measure the quilt you might estimate that it will finish at 72½", but the actual size may end up to be 72" or 73". The actual size may vary by a fraction of an inch higher or lower than the estimated size.

3   Determine the number of scallops on a quilt side. This requires math. Divide the estimated finished length of the quilt by the desired size of the scallop repeat.

The total length of the scallops should be close to the size of the finished edge. I recommend that the total scallop measurement not exceed a difference of ½" longer or shorter than the finished measurement of the finished quilt. If necessary, the measurement of the scallop edging may be larger or smaller than the quilt edge by more than ½", but as the difference increases, it becomes harder to fit the scallop edging to the quilt edge.

ADJUSTING SCALLOPS TO FIT THE QUILT EDGE

There are three ways to adjust the scallops to fit the quilt edge. Realistically, fitting the scallops to the quilt edge requires a combination of these methods.

Adjust scallop size. Adjust the scallop size to fit the quilt edge more closely. Redraw the scallop, changing its radius. To ensure exact measurements for the scallop repeat, make a sample scallop edging for every adjustment.

Adjust quilt size. Adjust the finished quilt size to fit the scallop edging. Cut the edges longer or shorter, as necessary. Usually the adjustments to the width or length are under ½". This option is not a good choice on quilts with piecing to the edges or with exacting quilting patterns.

Ease scallops. Ease the scallop edging to fit the quilt. To make

easing a more simple task, alter the space between the finished scallops by cutting the scallop strips into single scallops. The scallops can be set closer together or spaced farther apart. The raw edges will be covered with the binding.

CHANGING NEEDLE POSITIONS TO MAKE SCALLOPS FIT

On rectangular quilts, either the long or the short sides of the quilt may not be evenly divisible by a single scallop size. You can use the three listed methods to fit in the repeats, or slightly alter the radius of the scallop to change the size of the repeat. The easiest way to accomplish this small change is by using needle positions. Don't change the location of the pivot point. Simply change needle positions. Use a left needle position to make the curve smaller, or a right needle position to make the curve larger. On large quilts even this small change can drastically affect the number of repeats per side. Best of all, the small changes are not readily apparent to the casual observer.

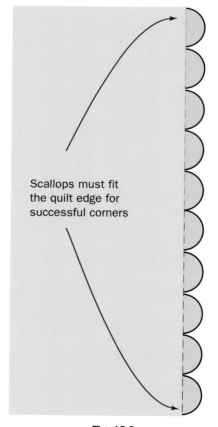

Scallops must fit the quilt edge for successful corners

Fig. 13-9

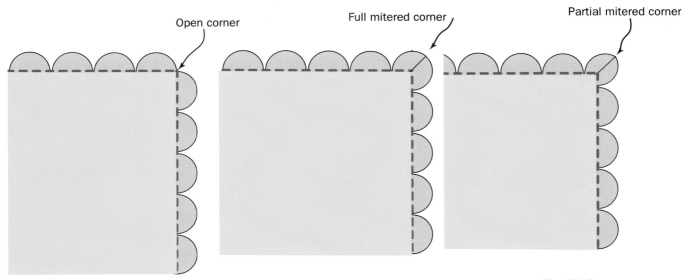

Open corner   Full mitered corner   Partial mitered corner

Fig. 13-10   **Fig. 13-11**   **Fig. 13-12**

SCALLOP CORNER OPTIONS

OPTION #1, OPEN CORNER

This is the simplest and most versatile corner. On this corner, the dip of the scallop falls at the exact corner. This precludes the need for a miter or turning the corners with the scallop edging. Two scallops simply meet at the corner. The binding covers the raw edges of the scallop edging. This corner requires whole scallop repeats. (See Fig. 13-10.)

OPTION #2, MITERED CORNER

Mitered corners are my favorite. The miter of the corner is on the crest of the scallop rather than at the dip. There are two types of mitered corners. On the full mitered corner, the scallop makes a three quarter circle (see Fig. 13-11). On the partial mitered corner, the scallop makes a shallow loop (see Fig. 13-12).

MITERING THE CORNERS OF THE SCALLOP FABRIC STRIPS

To turn a mitered corner requires a pre-stitched miter on each scallop corner strip. The basic shape and layout of the scallop strips should look like Figure 13-13. Note the corners are independent of the side strips. The side strips do not run

the entire length of the quilt. They abut the corner sections to complete the quilt edge. This method makes it easy to stitch and fit corners without working with yards of fabric strips at one time.

MAKING MITERED SCALLOP BINDING

1 Follow the basic steps for fitting the scallops (see page 125).

2 Cut, join, and fold the strips

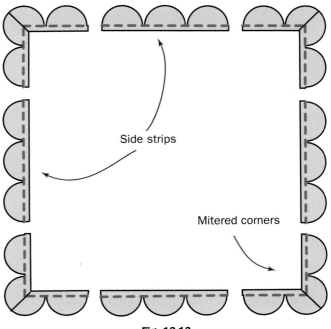

Side strips

Mitered corners

Fig. 13-13

required to make the four side strips. I suggest the strips measure the entire length of each side. The excess can be easily trimmed away prior to fitting to the quilt. Stitch the scallop on these strips.

3 Cut and fold the eight short strips needed to make the mitered corner. Each strip should be at least five times the length of the scallop repeat.

4 Unfold the strips. Place two strips right sides together, lining up the raw edges of the strips.

5 Using the center fold of the strips, mark the mitered corners. Use a ruler with a marked 45˚ angle. Place the 45˚ line along the center fold of the strips. At one end of the strip, draw the miters from the fold to within $\frac{1}{2}$" from the long straight edges of the strip (see Fig. 13-14). It is important that the miter seam be left unstitched $\frac{1}{2}$" from the raw edges. The unstitched sections are needed

to join the scallop corner to the quilt corner.

6 Stitch the mitered corner. Backstitch at the beginning and end of the miter. Trim the miter seam allowances to $\frac{1}{4}$" and press open the miter seam (see Fig. 13-15). Refold the strips. *Do not turn the strips right side out.* The mitered seam allowances must be visible. Line up the mitered seams and pin them together.

7 Using a fabric marker, mark the $\frac{1}{2}$" guideline along the fabric edges of the corner section. Mark the full corner or partial corner.

8 Cut the interfacing strip to match the miter. Do not seam a traditional seam. Butt the two raw edges of the miter together and stitch with a wide zigzag or mending stitch (see Fig. 13-16). Stop stitching $\frac{1}{2}$" before the inside edge.

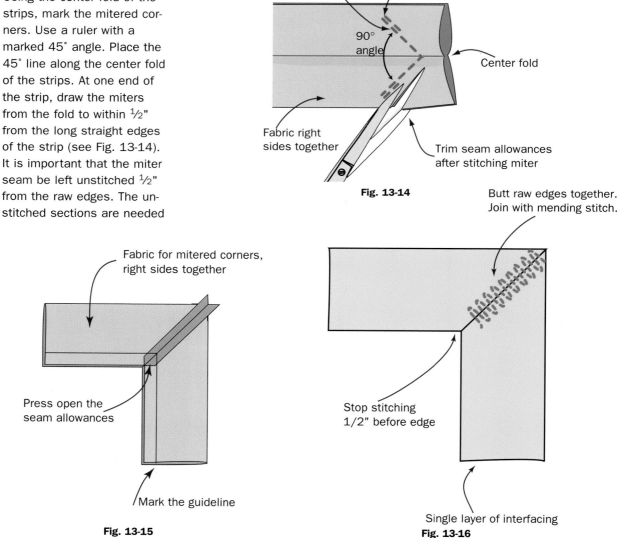

Stop and start miter
1/2" from strip edge

Stitch miter

90°
angle

Center fold

Fabric right
sides together

Trim seam allowances
after stitching miter

Fig. 13-14

Fabric for mitered corners,
right sides together

Press open the
seam allowances

Mark the guideline

Fig. 13-15

Butt raw edges together.
Join with mending stitch.

Stop stitching
1/2" before edge

Single layer of interfacing

Fig. 13-16

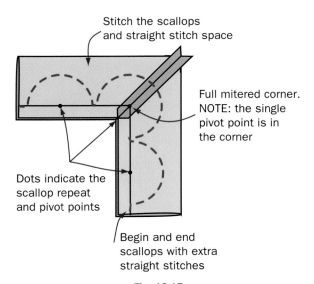

Stitch the scallops and straight stitch space

Full mitered corner. NOTE: the single pivot point is in the corner

Dots indicate the scallop repeat and pivot points

Begin and end scallops with extra straight stitches

Fig. 13-17

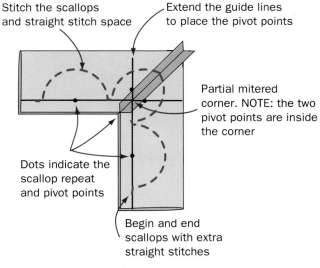

Stitch the scallops and straight stitch space

Extend the guide lines to place the pivot points

Partial mitered corner. NOTE: the two pivot points are inside the corner

Dots indicate the scallop repeat and pivot points

Begin and end scallops with extra straight stitches

Fig. 13-18

FULL MITERED CORNER

In the full mitered corner the scallops form a three quarter circle. In Figure 13-17, note how the pivots of the scallops line up with the edges of the quilt. The pivots for the scallop fall on the exact corner.

1 Starting at the exact corners of lines, mark two scallop repeats along each side of the corner strip. These marks indicate the center or pivot point for the scallops and will ensure the scallop repeats accurately fit the mitered corner.

2 Stitch the entire scallop corner. I suggest you begin and end the corner with a few

extra straight stitches in the straight stitch spacer. The extra straight stitches make the corner easier to turn right side out and fit to the quilt. Note the mitered corner is not a half circle, but three quarters of a circle.

3 Trim and turn the corner right side out. Mark and cut the straight edge with a ¼" seam allowance.

Note: The scallop repeat for the quilt edge is measured using whole repeats.

PARTIAL MITERED CORNER

In the partial mitered corner the scallops form a shallow loop

formed by two overlapping scallops. Note in Figure 13-18 how the pivots of the scallops line up with the edges of the quilt. The pivots for the corner fall beyond the quilt corner. The amount of the offset of the pivots determines the size of the loop. The most pleasing loops are offset one third of the scallop radius.

1 Determine the offset amount by dividing the radius of the scallop by three. In Figure 13-19 the scallop radius is ¾". Divided by three, it equals ¼".

2 Extend the corner guidelines into the strips. Measuring along the extended guideline, measure ¼" out from each

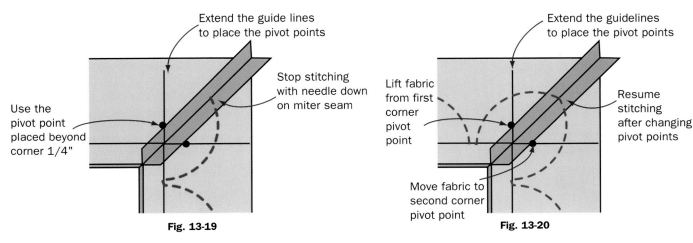

Extend the guide lines to place the pivot points

Use the pivot point placed beyond corner 1/4"

Stop stitching with needle down on miter seam

Fig. 13-19

Extend the guidelines to place the pivot points

Lift fabric from first corner pivot point

Resume stitching after changing pivot points

Move fabric to second corner pivot point

Fig. 13-20

corner and mark. This marks the pivot points for the corner scallops.

3 Starting at the corner pivot, mark two scallop repeats along each side of the corner strips.

4 Begin stitching the mitered corner. I suggest you begin and end the corner with a few extra straight stitches in the straight stitch spacer. The extra straight stitches make the corner easier to turn right side out and fit to the quilt. Stitch to the corner scallop. Note the corner scallops stop at the mitered seam. Stop stitching with needle lowered into the fabric on the seam-line.

5 Raise the presser foot. Lift the fabric off the pivot point of the circle maker. Realign the fabric to the second pivot point. Lower the presser foot and continue to stitch.

6 Trim and turn the corner right side out. Mark and cut the straight edge with a ¼" seam allowance.

Note: This corner doesn't have full scallop repeats in the corners. To fit the scallops to the quilt requires planning for the partial scallop repeats in the quilt corner. The total scallop repeat for the quilt edge must include two-thirds of a repeat. In Figure 13-20, two-thirds of the 1¹/₂" repeat is 1". To determine the number of scallop repeats needed for each edge of this quilt, I subtracted 1" from the quilt length before dividing the remaining length by the scallop repeat of 1¹/₂".

STITCHING THE SCALLOP EDGING TO THE QUILT

Trim the quilt edge to the finished size plus a ¹/₄" seam allowance.

1 Cut the corners and the straight strips to end at a scallop spacer.

2 Mark the exact corner of the seam lines of the corner of the quilt.

3 Place the scallop corner and quilt wrong sides together. Place the base of the mitered seam directly over the corner mark on the quilt. Split the unstitched section of the corner to line up the raw edges of the scallop strip and the quilt. Stitch the scallop corners in place.

4 Place the wrong side of the scallop edging against the back of the quilt. To join the side scallops to the corner scallops, simply butt the corner scallop to a side scallop to form a complete edge. The join is not stitched, simply placed side by side.

5 Line up the raw edges of the scallop strip and the

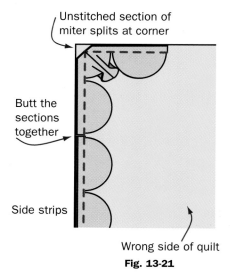

Unstitched section of miter splits at corner

Butt the sections together

Side strips

Wrong side of quilt

Fig. 13-21

quilt. Pin the edging to the quilt. Stitch the scallop edging to the quilt sides. When stitching, stretch or ease the scallop edge to match the quilt edge.

6 Bind the quilt using a mock binding (see page 107).

SCALLOP OPTION #2: GENTLE CURVE SCALLOP

These alternative circle maker scallops are an advanced method. The scallop method that used the circle maker on page 122 resulted in a half circle scallop. The circle maker can also make a more gentle curve. The trick is to use two lines for each scallop instead of a single line. There is a pivot line and a guideline. By placing the pivot line below the guideline, you stitch only a small portion of the circle rather than a half circle.

To determine the fabric strip width for this scallop edging, measure twice the radius of the circle plus 2".

1 In Figure 13-22, the pivot line is ½" below the guide. I chose to make the radius of the scallop 1". The pivot point was placed 1" to the left of the needle.

2 To start the scallop, line up the pivot line with the pivot point. Press the fabric to the point.

3 Line up the guideline under the needle. Stitch the scallop from guideline to guideline.

4 Remove the fabric from the pivot point, and make the straight stitch spacer between the scallops.

5 Repeat the basic steps for using the circle maker on

page 123–124 to complete the scallops. Determine the measure of the scallop repeat by measuring the sample scallop edging.

6 An open corner for gently curved scallops is the simplest (see Fig. 13-24). The other corner choice is the partial miter (see Fig. 13-25). Figure 13-26 shows the pivot point layout for a partial

mitered corner. Note the pivot points for the corners are located where the extended pivot lines intersect the guidelines. This partial corner requires full scallop repeats to fit the quilt.

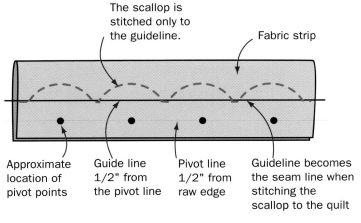

The scallop is stitched only to the guideline.

Fabric strip

Approximate location of pivot points

Guide line 1/2" from the pivot line

Pivot line 1/2" from raw edge

Guideline becomes the seam line when stitching the scallop to the quilt

Fig. 13-22

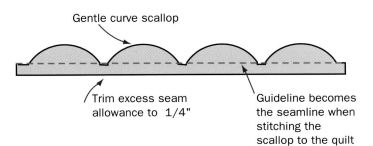

Gentle curve scallop

Trim excess seam allowance to 1/4"

Guideline becomes the seamline when stitching the scallop to the quilt

Fig. 13-23

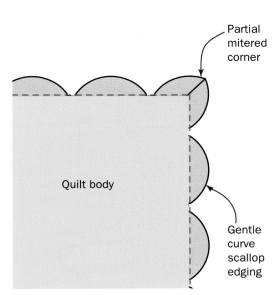

Partial mitered corner

Quilt body

Gentle curve scallop edging

Fig. 13-25

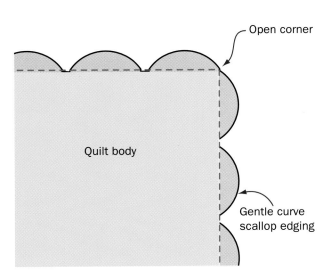

Open corner

Quilt body

Gentle curve scallop edging

Fig. 13-24

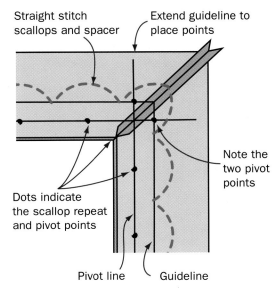

Straight stitch scallops and spacer

Extend guideline to place points

Dots indicate the scallop repeat and pivot points

Note the two pivot points

Pivot line

Guideline

Fig. 13-26

I like the appearance of the curves and corners when the distance between the pivot line and guideline is equal to half the radius of the circle. In Figure 13-27, a 1" radius results in a distance of $^1/_2$" between the lines. The biggest concern with the gentle scallop is the size of the scallop repeat. With the basic line ratio of the distance between lines is equal to half the radius, a simple math formula will tell you the approximate size of each scallop. The radius times 1.732 equals the scallop size:

Distance between lines x 2 = radius

Radius x 1.732 = scallop size

Advanced Methods: The basic line ratio is totally arbitrary. Changing the ratio between the two lines and the radius of the circle gives many variations of curves and corners. The pivot line can even be placed above the guideline. With the pivot line above the guideline the curves become more circular. To list the strip widths and line placement for every variation would be an impossible task. I suggest you draw out sample scallop edgings on paper using a compass and rotary ruler. Next, make a sample strip to determine the strip width and line placement required for your choice of curve.

The gold example in the center is a classic wave binding with piped mock binding. The green examples are all shallow scallop binding. The shallow scallop offers the most variations. The center examples show corner possibilities: at bottom right is an open corner, at top right is a partial miter corner. The green examples on the left show the shallow scallop binding on a smaller scale. All the examples are bound with piped mock binding.

FITTING SCALLOP TO QUILT EDGE

The next problem is fitting the scallop to the quilt edge. All curves require some fine tuning to fit the edge correctly. The easiest way to make *small* changes in the scallop size is to move the pivot line slightly closer or farther away from the guideline. Don't change the radius, just the pivot line. The closer the pivot and guidelines, the larger the scallop. The greater the distance between the pivot and guidelines the smaller the scallop. The same effect can be accomplished by changing the needle position. Use the left needle position to make the curve larger; the right needle position to make the curve smaller.

SCALLOP OPTION #3: THE SCALLOP WAVE

Unlike the previous scallop edgings, the wave is made from two gentle curves. This scallop uses two pivot points to make opposing curves. The pivot point for the outer curve is to the left of the needle. The pivot point for the inner curve is to the right of the needle. I always use thumbtacks for this scallop, but the long point of a regular tack affects the feeding of the fabric. I use a metal grinder to shorten both tack points to about one half of the original length.

 Hot Tip

I use shortened thumb tacks for all my scallop edgings. They work so much better than regular tacks. Simply place your finger over the slight point and pivot the fabric.

The gentle curves of the wave have identical radii. The three lines required for the wave are a centered guideline flanked by two pivot lines. Stitch the curves by pivoting around opposite pivot points. The size of the scallop repeat is the combined measure of the inner and outer curves.

Like the previous scallop, these directions use the basic line ratio for gentle curve: the distance between pivot lines and the guideline is equal to half the radius. This ratio makes determining the strip width and layout reasonably simple. Other ratios will work, but I leave the math to you.

To determine the fabric strip width required for this scallop, measure twice the radius of the circle plus 3".

1 Prepare the strips following basic instructions (see page 121).

2 Begin marking on the raw edge. Measuring from that edge, mark in ¼" for the seam allowance used to join the edging to the quilt, then mark ½".

3 Draw the first line ½" from the raw edge. This is the seamline that joins the edging to the quilt.

4 Mark and draw the second line ½" from the first. This is the inner pivot line.

5 The third line is the guideline for the scallops and should be half the radius from the second line. In Figure 13-27 that is ½" from the second line.

6 The fourth line is the outer pivot line. It is the same distance from the guideline as the guideline is from the inner pivot line. In Figure 13-27 it is ½".

7 Stitch the scallops by alternating the pivot points. Except for mitered corners, the pivot points do not need to be marked. Always stop with the needle lowered in the fabric before moving to the next point. This ensures the scallops are a smooth line of stitching.

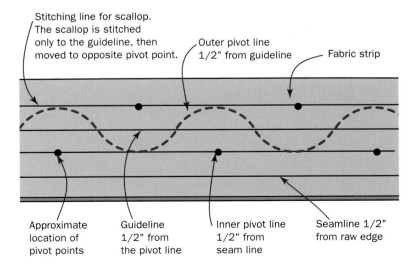

Fig. 13-27

8 The best corner choice for this variation is the full mitered corner. This makes an exaggerated loop on the corner that accentuates your cornering skills. Figure 13-30 shows the location of the pivot point for this corner.

The wave scallop poses some unique ways to deal with corners and fitting the scallops to the quilt. In this edging the inner curves sit $1/2$" from the binding edge. The extra width improves the appearance of the edging, but changes how the scallop fits the quilt. In the previous scallops the seamline fell on the guideline. This edging is measured completely differently. The seamline is $1/2$" below the pivot line. Although it sounds confusing, it is simple to determine the number of scallop repeats required on each quilt side. Add 1", for the two extra $1/2$" widths, to the quilt measure. Divide this number by the repeat measure to determine the number of repeats per side.

The extra width also changes how the mitered corners join the side edging. Simply butting the raw edges won't work. The join has

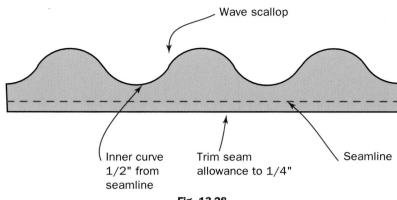

Wave scallop

Inner curve 1/2" from seamline

Trim seam allowance to 1/4"

Seamline

Fig. 13-28

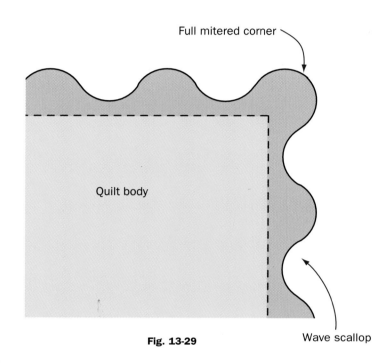

Full mitered corner

Quilt body

Wave scallop

Fig. 13-29

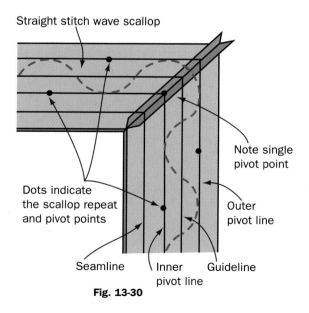

Straight stitch wave scallop

Note single pivot point

Dots indicate the scallop repeat and pivot points

Outer pivot line

Seamline

Inner pivot line

Guideline

Fig. 13-30

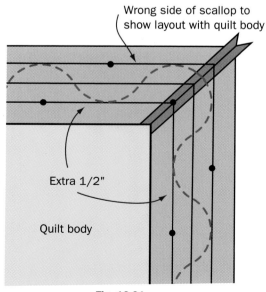

Wrong side of scallop to show layout with quilt body

Extra 1/2"

Quilt body

Fig. 13-31

to be stitched. The simplest way is to straight stitch the edgings together on an inner curve. Open the edging. The outer curves will pleat in the center of the strip. Only the inner curves are flat. Place two strips right sides together. Join the strips by straight stitching across the midpoint of the inner curve. Stitch the seam perpendicular to the edging, or on the bias. Trim the seam allowance, press and turn the edging right side out.

OTHER METHODS FOR MAKING SCALLOPS

The following three methods offer other ways to make scallops. The directions give a general explanation of the methods. The only directions given for mitered corners use the circle maker method given on pages 122–124. The circle maker is the easiest method for laying out full or partial mitered corners. Once mastered, the principles of corner layout apply to any style of corner.

Note: Making mitered corners on the optional scallop methods can be difficult. I know it is possible to do a true mitered corner on any scallop, but these skills are difficult to explain in the simple repeatable steps required for good directions. On these scallop edges I believe successful full mitered corners are a combination of advanced quilting skills and luck, rather than step-by-step directions.

SCALLOP OPTION #4: DRAW THE SCALLOP ONTO A STRIP OF FABRIC

This is the most traditional method.

1 Fold the fabric strip, right sides together.

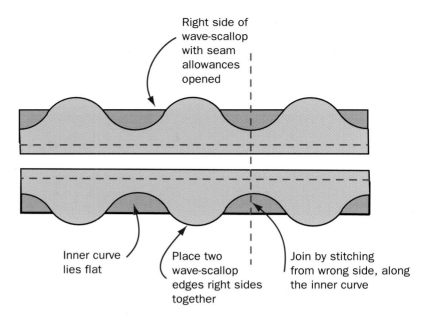

Right side of wave-scallop with seam allowances opened

Inner curve lies flat

Place two wave-scallop edges right sides together

Join by stitching from wrong side, along the inner curve

Fig. 13-32

2 Make a cardboard or plastic template of the scallop pattern and trace it onto one side of the fabric strip.

3 Straight stitch on the marked line. The basic strip measures twice the depth of the scallop plus 2".

4 Clip and turn the scallop.

5 After completing the scallops, trim the raw edge seam allowance to ¼".

6 Stitch the scallop edging to the quilt and finish with mock binding.

Advantages:
- ❏ Gives you a wide variety of scallop sizes.
- ❏ Both the width and depth can be adjusted.
- ❏ The scallop can be oval rather than circle based.

Disadvantages:
- ❏ Is the slowest, most time-intensive method of making scallops.

SCALLOP OPTION #5: USING A DECORATIVE STITCH TO MAKE THE SCALLOP

This is the least traditional method to make the scallop, and the only method without a turned edge. An automatic stitch that stitches a scallop forms the scallop edging. See photo on page 136 for possible stitches.

The basic strip measures twice the depth of the scallop plus 2".

1 Fold the fabric strip wrong sides together, with the interfacing sandwiched between the top and bottom strip. Using a fabric marker, mark a straight line ½" from the fabric edge. When joining the scallops to the quilt, stitch along this line.

2 Stitch the entire length of the strip. Cut the scallop along the stitching line. Cut as close as possible to the stitching line without cutting the stitches. Use Fray Check to repair any clipped stitches.

3 After completing the scallops, trim the raw edge seam allowance to ¼".

4 Stitch the scallop edging to the quilt and finish with mock binding.

Advantages:

❏ Very fast method to make the scallops.

❏ Gives a decorative edge to the scallop.

Disadvantages:

❏ Limited style and size of scallop.

❏ Readily apparent that the stitching is machine done.

❏ The cut edge of the scallop is weaker than the traditional turned edges. It may lose its shape with handling or washing.

 **Hot Tip**

Simple decorative stitches can be combined with the circle maker to make decorative stitched scallops. Use satin stitch or buttonhole stitch. Buttonhole stitch with decorative threads makes a great edge for felt or wool quilts.

A selection of decorative stitched scallops. Second from the top uses a scallop stitch on the sewing machine. The others use a decorative stitch combined with the circle maker. The scallops are shown with thread and the open toe embroidery foot.

SCALLOP OPTION #6: USING MULTIPLE DIRECTIONAL STITCHING

This method uses the multiple directional stitching feature and programmable memory on a computerized sewing machine. Multiple directional stitching is sometimes called eight way feed. This method also requires stitches that can be programmed into the machine's memory to repeat the scallop.

I have used these features on a number of computerized machines. I can't give detailed directions for every machine, but the basic directions apply to every machine with these features.

1 Determine the stitching sequence needed to stitch the scallop. The scallop can be any size or shape you wish. To make the pattern, use a compass and ruler to draw four or five scallops on scrap fabric backed with freezer paper. Mark the beginning, end, and midpoint of every scallop to maintain a correct width and depth. Choose straight stitch and the multiple directional stitching on your machine.

2 Experiment with the stitch directions and the number of stitches needed to duplicate the scallop. The scallop may be more squared then the drawing because of the limited number of directions the machine stitches. This is all right; the key to success is the uniformity of the scallops, not the exact shape.

⊛ Sewing Savvy

It is important that you note the direction and number of stitches as they are sewn. This will be the programming information. Sew scallops using different directions and numbers of stitches. Then choose the best scallop shape to program into memory.

3 Program the memory.

4 Layer the fabric strips right sides together. The strip measures twice the depth of the scallop plus 2". Using a fabric marker, mark a straight line ½" from the fabric edge. The scallops will be stitched to the quilt along this line.

5 Stitch the scallops.

6 Clip and turn the scallops. After completing the scallops, trim the raw edge seam allowance to ¼".

7 Stitch the scallop edging to the quilt and finish with mock binding.

Advantages:
❑ This method looks like the traditional method without the hassle of hand guiding around all the curves.

❑ The machine quickly repeats the curves.

❑ The machine can be programmed to do a variety of scallop sizes, both in width and height.

❑ The scallop can be altered to less traditional shapes.

Disadvantages:
❑ The machine-guided scallops can be slightly squared as compared to the hand-guided scallops.

❑ Requires a machine with these special features.

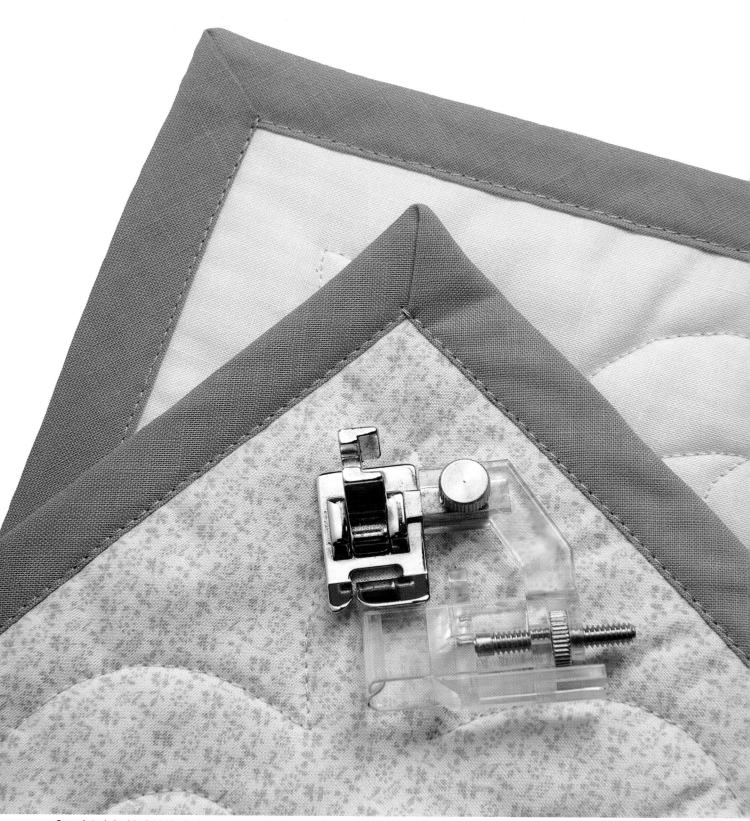

Completed double-fold binding shown from the right and wrong sides. The print side is the right side. In case you're curious, I didn't cheat when I sewed the wrong side example: I topstitched the binding from the right side. It shows the kind of accuracy possible with double-fold binding. Shown with a binding foot, but the example was made with prefolded tape and using an edgestitch foot.

CHAPTER 14
Double-Fold Bindings and Bias Binders

IN THE EARLY 1970S, I started using double-fold bias tape on my sewing projects. My first experience with bias binding was with prepackaged double-fold bias tape. Back then the finished bias tape was a mere $1/4$" wide and sharply pressed into three folds. Double-fold bias tape could be used with or without a bias binder and always gave great results. It looked neat and worked so well, I was in love with binding. Soon I was making my own double-fold tapes in a variety of fabrics and widths. I remember binding everything in sight: cosmetic bags, quilted vests, and even using it as a decorative edge finish on wool, linen, and silk garments. It wasn't until I became involved in quilt making that I realized many quilters didn't share my love affair with double-fold binding.

After all this time, I still think double-fold bias binding is the fastest way to bind a quilt. The problems commonly encountered with double-fold binding are not in the design of the binding. Rather, they're in the preparation and application of the binding. Learning to make and use double-fold bias binding opens the door to a new way to bind quilts.

BASIC DOUBLE-FOLD BIAS BINDING

Double-fold bias binding works best with finished binding widths in excess of $1/2$". Double-fold binding is the fastest and easiest way to bind a quilt, but does lack accuracy. Stitching both sides of the binding with a single line of stitching can result in less than perfect

stitching on the wrong side of the binding. I use and recommend double-fold binding for utilitarian quilts, rather than heirlooms.

MAKING THE BINDING

1 Heavily starch all fabrics before cutting. The secret to this method is to use heavy starch when preparing the

fabric. The starch maintains the width of the folded strip. The heavier the starch, the easier it is to make the binding and to bind the quilt.

2 Cut the bias or straight strip. To determine the strip size multiply the finished width of the binding by four. Make the cut width generous, and add an extra $\frac{1}{8}$".

Finished Width	Cut Size
$\frac{1}{2}$"	$2" + \frac{1}{8}" = 2\frac{1}{8}"$
$\frac{5}{8}$"	$2\frac{1}{2}" + \frac{1}{8}" = 2\frac{5}{8}"$
$\frac{3}{4}$"	$3" + \frac{1}{8}" = 3\frac{1}{8}"$

3 Stitch the bias strips together on the short ends to make a single long length of bias. Press all seams open. Press carefully. Do not stretch the bias edges.

FOLDING THE BINDING

Fold the strips of fabric by pulling the strip under two pins. The pins roll in the raw edges to form the first two folds; the third fold is done in a separate step. This method requires two long straight pins like corsage pins, a 12" square of heavy muslin, ruler, rotary cutter and mat, hemostat and a good steam iron.

1 The muslin square will be used as a pattern and to protect the ironing board cover. Fold the muslin square in half to make a double layer. On one side of the muslin draw two parallel lines 6" long, equal to twice the finished width of the binding plus $\frac{1}{8}$". These lines can be drawn with any fine line marker.

Finished Width	First Fold Size
$\frac{1}{2}$"	$1\frac{1}{8}$"
$\frac{5}{8}$"	$1\frac{3}{8}$"
$\frac{3}{4}$"	$1\frac{5}{8}$"

2 Fold in a seam allowance on each edge of the strip. The folded strip will measure approximately one-half the cut size of the strip. The cut edges do not touch, but almost meet in the center of the folded strip. Fold the strip with the right side out. Fold for about an inch. Crease the folds with your fingers and press with the iron.

3 Place one pin in the muslin on one end of the drawn lines. The pin is perpendicular to the lines. The pin goes into the muslin a short distance from the line. Bring the pin out of the fabric on the first line. Place the folded end of the strip under the pin. The right side of the strip is against the muslin, raw edges up. Bring the pin across the strip and into the muslin on the second line.

The folded strip fits tightly under the pin.

4 Pin the muslin to the ironing board. Place pins on the corners of the muslin.

 **Caution**

The muslin must be pinned to the ironing board to prevent it from moving when you press the strip.

5 Pull about an inch of the strip under the pin. Grasp the folded end.

 **Hot Tip**

(In this case, a cool tip.) Grasp the folded edge of a strip being ironed with a hemostat. The hemostat protects your fingers from the heat and steam of the iron. Place the point of the iron on the folded strip. Do not place the iron over the pin. To turn the strip correctly you must be able to see the pin and where the folds are formed.

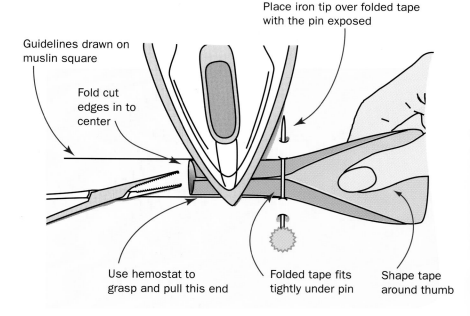

Place iron tip over folded tape with the pin exposed

Guidelines drawn on muslin square

Fold cut edges in to center

Use hemostat to grasp and pull this end

Folded tape fits tightly under pin

Shape tape around thumb

Fig. 14-1

6 With the iron in place, pull four inches of fabric under the pin. Hold the unfolded strip, slightly elevated, in your right hand. Place your thumb in the center of the strip about two inches from the pin. Use your fingers to curve the edges of the strip up on either side of your thumb. This gentle curve keeps the strip folding evenly. It is important that the folded edges be even, almost touching in the center of the folded strip.

 **Caution**

Watch out for the steam. Don't place your fingers too close to the iron.

7 Remove the iron and place the folded end of the strip under a second pin. Place the second pin like the first, about three inches away from the first pin.

8 Place the iron in the space between the pins and continue pulling the strip. The iron is resting on the ironing board. It can scorch the ironing board cover. I recommend using a large muslin press cloth over the ironing board to protect the ironing board cover.

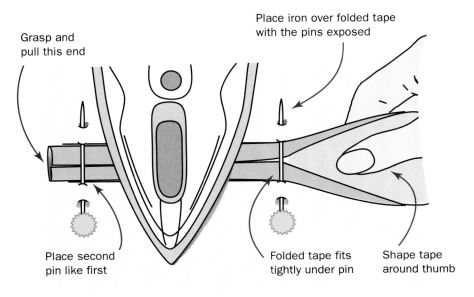

Grasp and pull this end

Place iron over folded tape with the pins exposed

Place second pin like first

Folded tape fits tightly under pin

Shape tape around thumb

Fig. 14-2

 **Hot Tip**

To make tapes faster, I recommend using Clover Bias Tape Makers. They make tape in two widths that are suitable for this method: 2" and 1".

MAKING THE THIRD FOLD

The third fold makes this tape double-fold. Use the same basic method used to make the first two folds.

Fold the prefolded strip approximately in half. It is important that one side of the tape be about $1/16$" wider than the other side. This extra wide side of the tape becomes the back of the binding and makes it easier to attach the binding with a single line of stitching. Fold the strip with the right side out. Fold for about an inch. Crease the folds with your fingers and press with

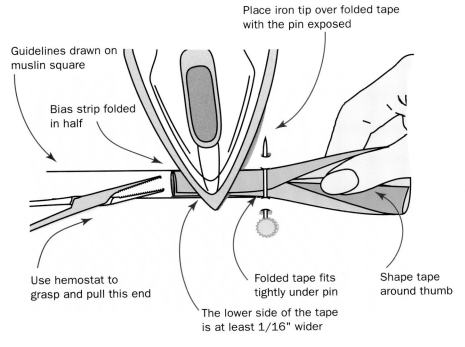

Guidelines drawn on muslin square

Bias strip folded in half

Place iron tip over folded tape with the pin exposed

Use hemostat to grasp and pull this end

Folded tape fits tightly under pin

Shape tape around thumb

The lower side of the tape is at least 1/16" wider

Fig. 14-3

the iron. Continue with the basic directions on page 140, starting with step #3.

PREPARING THE QUILT FOR BINDING

Before binding the quilt, trim the quilt to the finished size (including width of the finished binding). Set your machine for a medium length, widest-width zigzag to overcast the edges of the quilt. This overcast flattens the edge of the quilt and ensures a flat, smooth, and even binding.

STITCHING THE DOUBLE-FOLD BINDING TO THE QUILT

The best part of double-fold binding is that it requires only one line of stitching. Topstitching on the right side secures both edges of the binding. It's fast and simple.

 Sew A Sample

DOUBLE-FOLD BINDING SAMPLE

Supplies
- Binding as prepared earlier

Machine Setup

Straight stitch with an average stitch length

Open toe embroidery foot or edge stitching foot

Use an open toe embroidery foot or edge stitching foot to stitch the binding to the quilt. A number of feet can be used for edge stitching, including an edgestitch foot and blind hem foot. These feet are some of many feet with a metal or plastic guide. The guide rides along the edge of the fabric and ensures perfectly placed top-

stitching. Any foot works that allows you to evenly guide on the left of the finished edge and stitch on the right side of the finished edge. Frequently these feet require variable needle positions.

The thickness of the binding can make it difficult to hold the foot on the binding. A regular foot slips off the binding onto the thinner quilt body. Substitute a bulky fabric foot for the edgestitch foot. Guide the binding under the thinner portion of the foot, with the edge of the binding resting against the slight rise made by the thicker portion of the foot. This foot allows the extra thickness of the binding to feed smoothly, plus the rise in the foot acts as an edge stitching foot. Frequently these feet require variable needle positions to correctly align the straight stitch on the binding edge.

DOUBLE-FOLD BINDING WITH MITERED CORNERS

STARTING THE BINDING

1 Start the binding in the corner to make the neatest possible join. The miter is the perfect place to conceal the seam that will join the two ends of binding.

2 Begin by marking a miter on the wrong side of the binding beginning. Unfold the center fold of the binding end. Do not unfold the outer folds of the binding.

3 About 3" from the end of the binding mark the mitered corner. Use a ruler with a 45° angle mark. Place the 45° line on the center fold. Using a fabric marker, mark the mitered corner from the folded edges to the center fold.

4 Place the binding over the raw edge of the quilt. Put the widest side of the binding on the back of the quilt, the narrowest side on top. Line up the edge of the quilt against the outer fold of the binding. Line up the outside

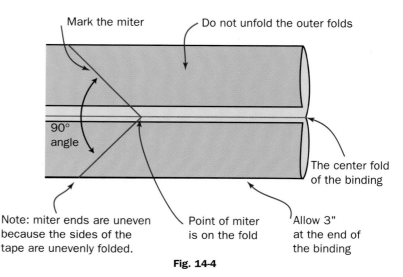

Mark the miter — Do not unfold the outer folds

90° angle

The center fold of the binding

Note: miter ends are uneven because the sides of the tape are unevenly folded.

Point of miter is on the fold

Allow 3" at the end of the binding

Fig. 14-4

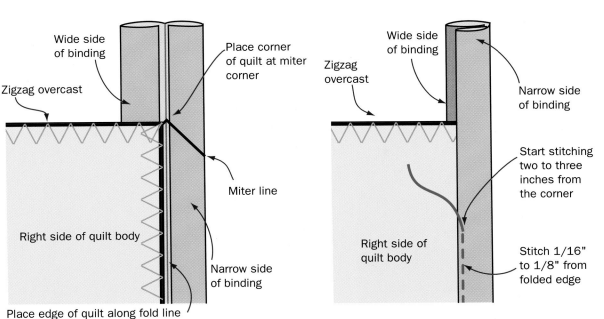

Fig. 14-5

Fig. 14-6

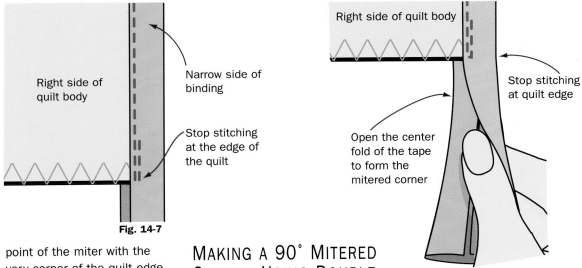

Fig. 14-7

Fig. 14-8

point of the miter with the very corner of the quilt edge. Slide the quilt edge into the double-fold binding. Fold the top of the binding in place. Pin to secure.

5 Start stitching on the right side of the quilt, 2" to 3" from the corner. Stitch the binding, stitching $\frac{1}{16}$" to $\frac{1}{8}$" in from the folded edge (see Fig. 14-6). Correctly done, the topstitching is a straight neat line on the top of the quilt. From the wrong side of the quilt the stitching catches the back binding $\frac{1}{16}$" deeper than the stitching on the front binding.

MAKING A 90° MITERED CORNER USING DOUBLE-FOLD BINDING

1 Stitch until reaching the very edge of the quilt. Backstitch and break threads. Remove the quilt from the machine.

2 Open the center fold of the binding and fold the binding around the corner. The miter simultaneously folds on both the front and the back of the quilt. Press the miter in place. Secure the miter with a pin, a dot of glue, or a hand basting stitch.

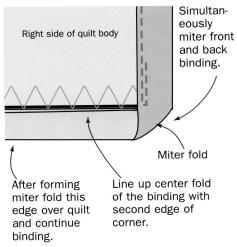

Fig. 14-9

3 For the least conspicuous start and knot, begin stitching at least ⅛" after the mitered corner. The first few stitches are in reverse, stitching backwards toward the exact mitered corner. Then stitch forward to complete binding.

ENDING THE BINDING

Continue stitching and mitering corners around the quilt. Stop stitching 2" to 3" before reaching the beginning corner. Backstitch to secure the stitching line. Remove the quilt from the machine. Cut the end of the binding to extend 3" beyond the edge of the quilt.

JOINING THE BINDING ENDS WITH A MITERED CORNER

1 Determine the exact corner of the binding end by lining up the end to the quilt and marking the very outside corner of the quilt with a pin. Pin into the center fold of the binding. The pin marks the outer point of the miter on the binding end.

2 Unfold the center fold of both binding ends. Do not unfold the outer folds of the binding.

3 Place the two binding ends right sides together. Line up the pin marking the outer point of the miter on the end of the binding and the outer point of the marked miter (that you marked earlier—see page 142). Line up the folded edges of the bindings. I recommend novices pin to secure the folded edges.

4 Stitch the mitered corner starting at the folded edge of the binding. Make sure the folded edges are exactly lined

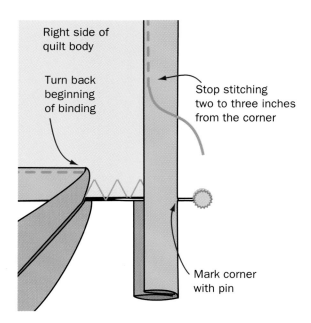

Right side of quilt body

Turn back beginning of binding

Stop stitching two to three inches from the corner

Mark corner with pin

Fig. 14-10

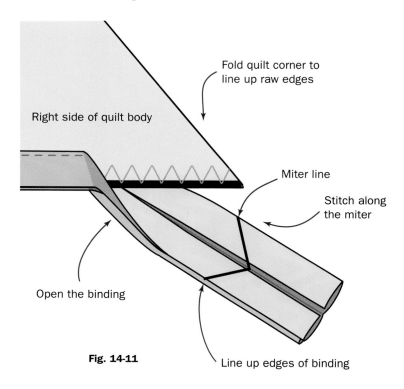

Fold quilt corner to line up raw edges

Right side of quilt body

Miter line

Stitch along the miter

Open the binding

Fig. 14-11

Line up edges of binding

up. To make a neat start, begin stitching about ¼" into the binding, then reverse to the folded edge and stitch forward to complete the miter. Stitch toward the outer point of the miter.

Sewing Savvy

The outer point of the miter is extremely sharp. This sharp point doesn't make a good finished corner. To make a great corner, shorten the point by taking one stitch across the point rather than stitching into the exact point.

5 Stitch to the first fold line. Backstitch to secure. Trim the seam allowances and press open the miter seam.

FINISHING THE BINDING

1 Turn the binding over the raw edges of the quilt to the front.

2 Pin the binding in place.

3 Stitch the corner to complete the binding.

OPTIONS FOR STITCHING BINDING TO THE QUILT

BLINDHEM STITCH OR OVERLOCK STITCH

The blindhem or overlock stitch is the perfect stitch to use with double-fold binding. For the least conspicuous topstitching, use blindhem or overlock stitches with invisible thread. On the quilt top, the straight stitches fall on the quilt body and only the zigzag stitch catches the binding edge. On the quilt back, both the straight stitch and small zigzag catch the binding. The stitch must be a straight stitch on the left and zigzag to the right. The stitch width should be as narrow as possible and yet catch the binding fabric. Use an edge stitch foot.

NARROW ZIGZAG STITCH

A narrow zigzag stitch combined with invisible thread is another choice for stitching the binding to the quilt. The zigzag stitch has the added advantage of a wider stitch width. The increased width ensures that both the front and back binding edges are caught in the stitching.

BIAS BINDERS

Bias binders are feet that attach bias binding to a fabric edge. Frequently overlooked, they have a reputation for being unsuitable for quilt making. When used correctly, these feet bind the quilt with only one line of stitching. Bias binders use single or double-fold bias binding. Their main purpose is to correctly guide the binding as it is stitched. They have advantages over the edge stitching foot. The binder ensures that the upper and *lower* edges are correctly placed, and binders have a wide center slot for easy guiding of the quilt edge.

There are two types of binders applicable to quilt making, a bed-mounted double-fold bias binder, and an adjustable bias binder.

Bed-Mounted Double-Fold Bias Binder. The bed-mounted double-fold bias binder attaches to the machine with two securing screws that fasten to the needleplate or free arm. Copied from commercial binders, this accessory comes in a number of sizes with each size making only one size of binding. This binder uses unfolded fabric strips or pre-folded binding.

The secret to using this attachment is that you should place the free end of the binding behind the

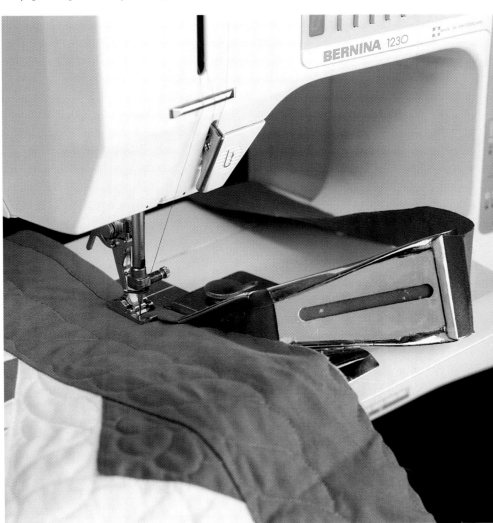

Bed type binder in use. This is a single size binder, using 2" bias strips, and resulting in approximately ½" binding. Note how the unfolded bias tape is curved toward the back of the machine. Also notice the distance between the binder and the presser foot. A half inch or more between the binder and foot results in better binding.

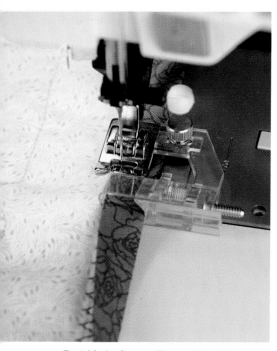

Foot binder in use. The prefolded bias tape is fed into the foot. The foot is adjusted to the width of the bias, using the silver screw on the right side of the foot.

foot. That way the flow of the binding matches the curve of the binder and feeds smoothly.

Adjustable Bias Binder. The adjustable bias binder is a generic presser foot. It has a plastic adjustable guide that will accept any size tape. Less expensive than the bed-mounted bias binder, the adjustable bias binder produces slightly less accurate results. This binder uses double-fold binding.

Hold the free end of the binding in front of the foot to ensure the binding falls in the curves of the binder and feeds smoothly.

APPLYING DOUBLE-FOLD BINDING USING A BIAS BINDER FOOT

Apply the basic double-fold directions in using the bias binder (see page 139). I recommend you use a finished binding width of $^{1}/_{2}$" or wider. The design of the foot makes it impossible to backstitch, or to remove the binding from the

foot. These changes affect the binding start, end, and corners.

STARTING THE BINDING USING A BINDER FOOT

1 Feed the bias binding into the binder. Set the sewing machine for the longest straight stitch. In this step you are sewing on just the binding, there is no other fabric. This step is to help you correctly line up the binding and the stitching line.

2 Stitch the binding for 3" to ensure the tape is properly feeding with the stitches correctly placed. Use the foot's adjustments or the sewing machine's needle positions to correctly place the stitches on the edge of the binding.

3 Without breaking the thread or cutting the binding, insert the quilt edge into the center slot. Start stitching at the quilt corner. Stitch for three inches using the long stitch length. The long stitches are a basting stitch. The basting stitches are needed later when joining the binding

ends. Use this step to make final adjustments to the feeding and stitching of the binding to the fabric. Do not break the threads or remove the quilt or binding from the machine.

4 Change the stitch length to average. Hold back the quilt and binding slightly, making tiny stitches that knot the threads. Continue to feed the quilt and binding normally along the straight edge.

MAKING A 90° MITERED CORNER USING A BIAS BINDER FOOT

1 Stitch until reaching the very edge of the quilt. Hold back the quilt and binding to knot the threads. Cut the threads. Because the quilt and binding cannot be removed from the foot, turn the corner at the machine (see page 143 to review miter folding).

2 Pull approximately 2" of binding and quilt through the binder. This excess turns the corner.

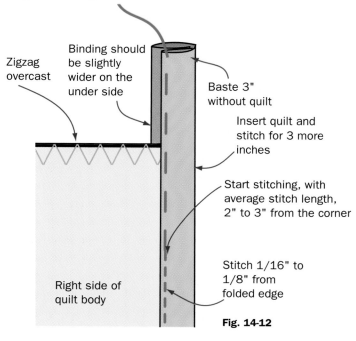

Zigzag overcast

Binding should be slightly wider on the under side

Baste 3" without quilt

Insert quilt and stitch for 3 more inches

Start stitching, with average stitch length, 2" to 3" from the corner

Stitch 1/16" to 1/8" from folded edge

Right side of quilt body

Fig. 14-12

Sewing Savvy

It is impossible to remove the binding from the presser foot, and turning the corner at the machine can be difficult. I recommend removing the foot, quilt, and binding from the machine and turning the corner at the ironing board. This lets you use an iron in pressing the corner, and results in a better miter. Simply take everything with you to the ironing board, or better yet, move the ironing board or pressing pad to the machine.

3 Open the center fold of the binding and fold the binding around the corner while placing the unbound side of the quilt in the center slot of the binder. The miter simultaneously folds on both the front and the back of the quilt (see page 143 to review miter folding). Finger press the miter in place. Heavily starched binding makes this step easier. Secure the miter with a pin or a single hand basting stitch.

4 Re-align the quilt edge and binding in the foot. (Replace the presser foot if you have removed it.) Pull the extra binding back into the binder until the mitered corner is under the needle. Hold back the fabric for the first few stitches to knot the threads. Then stitch forward to complete binding.

ENDING THE BINDING

1 Continue stitching around the quilt. Stop stitching 2" to 3" before reaching the beginning corner. Hold the fabric in place for a few stitches to knot the threads. To end the binding and prepare for the join requires basting stitches like were made at the binding start.

2 Change to the longest stitch length. Slowly pull the quilt out of the binder, so the stitching is only on the binding, without the quilt. Stitch the binding slowly off the quilt and continue to stitch on only the binding for about 6". The end of binding should extend about 3" beyond the corner of the quilt. Cut the threads and binding and remove the quilt from the machine.

JOINING THE BINDING ENDS WITH A MITERED CORNER

1 To determine the binding corners requires a firmly creased binding. I suggest you press the ends of the binding with a lot of steam and the iron set on the wool setting. Try not to press on the quilt body; press only the binding.

2 Determine the exact corner of the binding *start*. Mark the very outside corner of the quilt with a pin. Pin into the center fold. The pin marks the outer point of the miter on the binding end.

3 Rip the long stitches to remove the binding start from the quilt, without moving the pin. Remove the basting stitches on both free ends of the binding.

4 Determine the exact corner of the binding *end*. Slip the binding over the quilt edge.

Mark the very outside corner of the quilt with a pin. Pin into the center fold. The pin marks the outer point of the miter on the binding end.

5 Unfold the center fold. Do not unfold the outer folds of the binding.

6 Mark the miter on one end of the binding. Use a ruler with a 45° mark. Place the 45° line on the center fold with the point placed on the pin marking the corner. Using a fabric marker, mark the mitered corner from the folded edges to the center fold.

7 Place the binding ends right sides together. Line up the pins marking the outer points of the miters. Line up the folded edges. Pin to secure the folded edges.

8 Stitch the mitered corner starting at the finished edge of the binding. Make sure the finished edges are exactly lined up. To make a neat start, begin stitching about ¼" into the binding, then reverse to the finished edge and stitch forward to complete the miter. Stitch toward the outer point of the miter.

The outer point of the miter is extremely sharp. This sharp point doesn't make a good finished corner. To make a great corner, shorten the point by taking one stitch across the point rather than stitching into the exact point.

9 Stitch to the first stitching line. Backstitch to secure. Trim the seam allowances and press open the miter seam.

CHAPTER 15

Odds and Ends

AS QUILTERS, WE ALL KNOW the finishing work required on every quilt: odds and ends like adding rod pockets and name labels, and stitching the back seam on quilt-as-you-go quilts. Until now, this finishing has required hand stitching.

This chapter shows you how to do all these finishing details by machine. Most of the techniques are very easy and much faster than their hand counterparts. But these techniques have one drawback: they are more conspicuous than hand techniques. The stitching shows on the finished quilt. What the techniques lack in sophistication is more than compensated for by simplicity and speed. I'm the first to admit these methods may not be the best choice for heirloom or competition quilts, but many more quilts are made just for fun or use. These methods are the perfect choice for the "fun" quilts.

The directions for each of the following techniques list the basic machine setup and fabric preparation. Most methods are based on variations of the blindstitched hem used in garment construction. The methods work best with print fabrics that are medium to heavily starched.

MACHINE STITCHING A ROD POCKET

Use this technique on rod pockets enclosed by the binding.

On this style of pocket the top edge is under the binding, leaving only the bottom edge to be stitched in place. Hand stitching the bottom of the rod pocket is a pet peeve of mine. I stopped hand stitching this seam years ago when I discovered how to blind hem the pocket. The method is simple and strong. The trick is in stitching the bottom of the pocket to the quilt before stitching the top of the pocket into the binding. It seems backwards, but gives stunning results. Finally, the entire rod pocket can be machine stitched.

Sew A Sample

SAMPLE OF ROD POCKET

Supplies

• Make an 18" square quilt sandwich or use double-faced pre-quilted fabric

• Cotton fabric 10" x 18" for rod pocket

Machine Setup

Blindhem foot

Blindhem stitch with straight stitches on the right and a single zigzag to the left.

Set the stitch width and length to the setting recommended by your machine manufacturer for regular garment hemming.

MAKING THE ROD POCKET

1 Cut the rod pocket and hem the short edges. Fold the pocket in half the long way, wrong sides together and press. Do not stitch it to the top edge of the quilt.

2 Unfold the pocket. With right sides together line up the raw edges of the pocket and quilt back. Pin the single layer of the pocket to the top edge of the quilt. If desired, machine baste this seam.

3 Lay the upper portion of the quilt on a flat surface. Fold over the top of the quilt. The fold in the quilt should be at least ¹⁄₂" below the crease on the pocket. Smooth the pocket and pin along the fold in the quilt. Note the pins are perpendicular to the fold.

4 Stitch with the unfolded

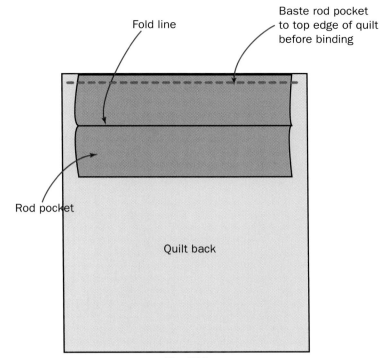

Fold line

Baste rod pocket to top edge of quilt before binding

Rod pocket

Quilt back

Fig. 15-1

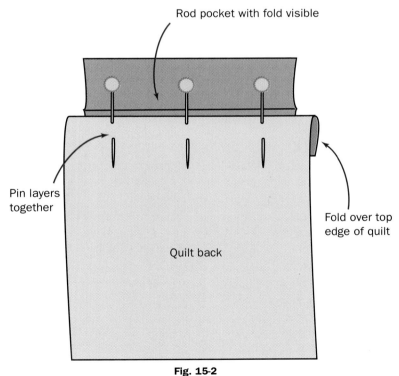

Rod pocket with fold visible

Pin layers together

Fold over top edge of quilt

Quilt back

Fig. 15-2

pocket on the bottom and the fold of the quilt on the top. The blind hem's straight stitch falls on the single layer of the pocket while the zigzag catches the fold of the quilt. Adjust the zigzag width to securely catch the quilt back without stitching through the batting. Use a simple zigzag stitch to secure the beginning and end of the line of stitches.

5 Unfold the quilt, and stitch the free side of the pocket to the top edge of the quilt.

6 Bind as desired.

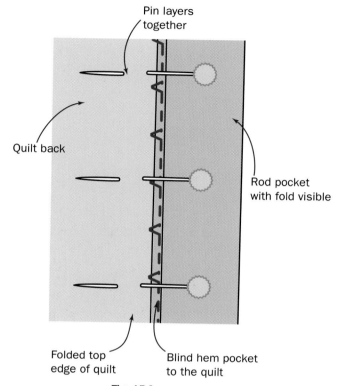

Pin layers together

Quilt back

Rod pocket with fold visible

Folded top edge of quilt

Blind hem pocket to the quilt

Fig. 15-3

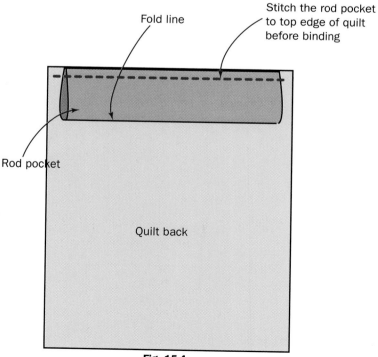

Fold line

Stitch the rod pocket to top edge of quilt before binding

Rod pocket

Quilt back

Fig. 15-4

STITCHING QUILT LABELS

Appliquéing the labels to quilt backs is my least favorite part of quilting. There are two easy ways to do this by machine. I recommend the buttonhole stitch but for those quilters without this stitch on their machine, I have also described the basic zigzag method.

STITCHING QUILT LABELS USING THE BUTTONHOLE STITCH METHOD

The buttonhole stitch appliqué technique makes a line of buttonhole stitches around the label. It is important that the label fabric be heavily starched, or for better results, turn the label edges over a Rinse Away template (see page 28). Use threads that match or complement the label color.

Fig. 15-5

 **Sew A Sample**

BUTTONHOLE STITCHED LABEL SAMPLE

Supplies

• Label, 4" square

• Rinse Away

• Previous quilt sample (from rod pocket section)
Note: Be sure to leave enough room on the quilt sample to try another label technique.

Machine Setup

Buttonhole stitch with the straight stitch on the right and the zigzag to the left

Stitch width set at about 1.5

Stitch length set at about 2.5

Center needle position

Slightly tightened needle tension

Open toe embroidery foot

Thread the bobbin and needle with matching thread.

Machine-stitched labels on quilt backs. The two examples on the left show zigzag-stitched labels. The label on the right is stitched with large stitches, in a mismatched thread so you can clearly see the stitch location. The label shown in Figures 15-5 to 15-8 is stitched using the buttonhole stitch. Although the stitches hold the labels to the back of the quilt, they are not visible on the right side of the quilt.

STITCHING THE LABEL

1 Make the label and fold under ½" seam allowances on all edges. Starch the label.

2 Pin the label to the wrong side of the quilt. Pin along the fold of the label. Note the pins are perpendicular to the fold. If desired, machine or hand baste the label in place. The basting should be ½" from the edge of the label.

3 Fold the quilt along one edge of the label. The folded edge of the quilt is ¹⁄₁₆" to ⅛" in from the folded edge of the label. It is important that the straight stitches be at a uniform distance from the edge of the label.

4 Stitch with the label on the bottom, the quilt on top.

5 Start stitching at the corner. Leave long thread tails to hand knot at the end of the stitching.

6 The straight stitch falls only on the label fabric, while the left stitch catches the fold of the quilt. Adjust the zigzag width to securely catch the quilt back without stitching through the batting.

7 Stitch to the corner and stop with the needle in the label. For the best corners see the detailed instructions for turning a corner with buttonhole stitch on page 77.

8 Pivot the quilt and label. Fold the quilt to line up with the next side of the label. Continue around the label.

9 Hand knot the thread tails on the first corner. Using a large hand sewing needle, pull the thread tails between the quilt label.

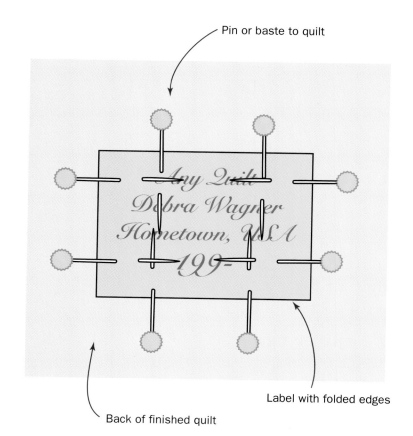

Pin or baste to quilt

Back of finished quilt

Label with folded edges

Fig. 15-6

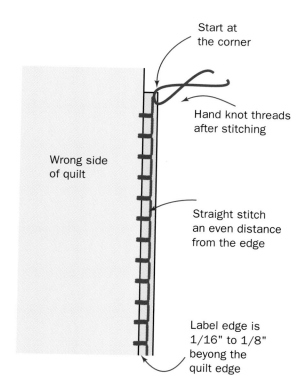

Start at the corner

Hand knot threads after stitching

Wrong side of quilt

Straight stitch an even distance from the edge

Label edge is 1/16" to 1/8" beyong the quilt edge

Fig. 15-7

STITCHING QUILT LABELS USING THE BASIC ZIGZAG METHOD

The zigzag appliqué technique appears as a double line of zigzag stitching around the label edge. For decorative effects use threads that match the quilt or the label, or use a third color.

Sew A Sample

ZIGZAG STITCH LABEL SAMPLE

Supplies

- Label, 4" square

- Rinse Away

- Previous quilt sample

Machine Setup

Zigzag stitch

Stitch width set at 1.5

Stitch length set at 1.0

Open toe embroidery foot or an edge stitch foot

Thread the needle and bobbin with matching thread

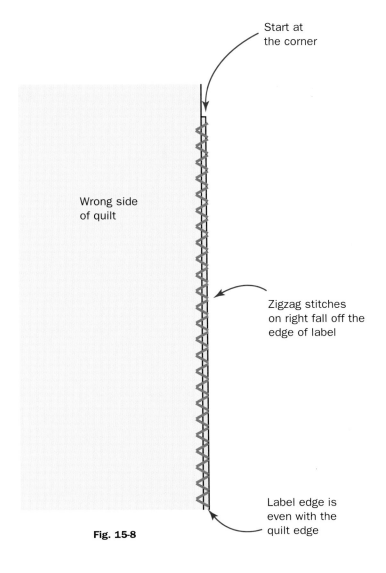

Start at the corner

Wrong side of quilt

Zigzag stitches on right fall off the edge of label

Label edge is even with the quilt edge

Fig. 15-8

STITCHING THE LABEL

1 Make the label and fold in ½" seam allowances on all the edges. Starch the label.

2 Pin the label to the quilt. Pin along the fold of the label. Note the pins are perpendicular to the fold (see Fig. 15-6). If desired, machine or hand baste the label in place. The baste should be ½" from the edge of the label.

3 Fold the quilt along the edge of the label. The folded edge of the quilt is along the folded edge of the label.

4 Stitch with the label on the bottom, the quilt on top.

5 Start stitching at the corner. Leave long thread tails to hand knot at the end of the stitching.

6 The right stitch falls off the fabrics, while the left stitch catches the fold of the quilt. Adjust the zigzag width to securely catch the quilt back without stitching through the batting.

7 Stitch to the corner and stop with the needle out of the fabrics. *Do not* cut the threads.

8 Pull the quilt from under the presser foot, until the quilt is at least three inches from the foot. Fold the quilt to line up with the next side of the label.

9 Loop the threads around your left fingers and slide the quilt and label under the foot. Pull the thread tails taut. Start stitching at the corner. Continue around the label.

10 Hand knot the thread tails on all four corners. Using a large hand sewing needle pull the thread tails between the quilt and the label.

MAKING BLIND SEAMS

Blind seams are the perfect choice for machine-joining the back seam of quilt-as-you-go blocks. I love this technique, because my machine stitch quality is much better than my hand stitching. Use the same technique to blind stitch binding to the quilt back when using traditional front-to-back binding methods or to blind stitch the quilt label.

The seam uses the blindhem stitch or an overlock variation (see page 145 in Chapter 14). I recommend using print fabrics and a fine thread that matches or blends with the surrounding fabrics.

Sew A Sample

BLIND SEAM SAMPLE: SEW TWO BLOCKS TOGETHER USING THE BLIND SEAM.

Supplies

• Two non-quilted 5" blocks of cotton

Machine Setup

Blindhem stitch or overlock variation. I recommend straight stitches on the right with a single zigzag to the left.

Stitch width set at 1.5

Stitch length set at 1.0

Center needle position

Open toe embroidery foot, an edge stitch foot, or a bulky fabric foot.

Slightly loosen the needle tension.

Thread the needle and bobbin with matching thread.

STITCHING THE BLIND SEAM

1 Fold in the seam allowances on the seam edges. This method is most successful with medium to heavily starched fabrics.

2 Place the seams wrong sides together and pin. The fold edges of the seams should be uniform. Place the pins perpendicular to the fold. If desired, machine baste the seams together. The basting should be ½" from the edges of the seam.

3 Start stitching at the end of the seam. Leave long thread tails to hand knot at the end of the stitching.

4 The straight stitch falls off the fabrics (in the air), while the zigzag catches the fold of the seams. Adjust the zigzag width to securely catch the seams with the smallest possible bite (see Fig. 15-9).

5 Leave long thread tails at the end of the seam for hand knotting. Using a large hand sewing needle pull the thread tails between the quilt back and batting.

 Hot Tip

If the blind seam doesn't lie flat, loosen the top tension. If you're having trouble catching the seams, loosening the top tension allows wider stitch widths to lie flat.

Blind stitched seams and binding. The example in the upper left is stitched with mismatched thread to show the stitch location. The quilted example is stitched with matching thread and shows the finished appearance of the seam. The binding example shows the right and wrong side of the quilt. Note the blind stitching is not visible on the right side of the quilt. The plain muslin is the right side of the quilt. The print is the quilt back. I used mismatched thread to blind stitch the binding in order to highlight the stitches. I suggest choosing a thread to match the binding, or using invisible thread for the actual binding.

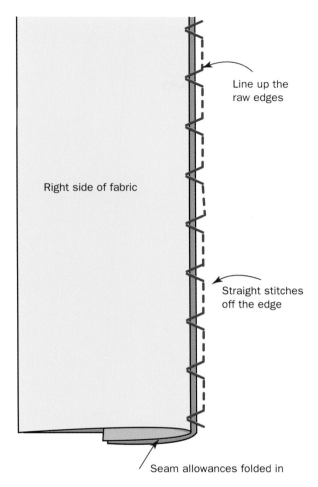

Line up the raw edges

Right side of fabric

Straight stitches off the edge

Seam allowances folded in

Fig. 15-9

BLIND STITCHING FOR BINDING OR QUILT LABELS

I recommend using print fabrics and a fine thread that matches or blends with the quilt backing fabric.

 Sew A Sample

BLIND STITCH LABEL SAMPLE

Supplies

To try a blind stitch sample, you need to have at least a 6" quilted square with French binding attached to the right side and turned, ready for the second stitching line.

Machine Setup

Blindhem stitch or overlock variation. I recommend two straight stitches on the right with a single zigzag to the left.

Stitch width set at 1.5

Stitch length set at 1.0

Center needle position

Use the open toe embroidery foot or an edge stitch foot.

Slightly loosen the needle tension.

Thread the needle and bobbin with matching thread.

BLIND-STITCHING THE BINDING

1 Pin the binding to the quilt back. Pin along the fold of the binding. Note the pins are perpendicular to the fold. If desired, machine or hand baste the binding in place. The basting should be ¼" from the edge of the binding.

2 Fold the quilt along the edge of the binding. The folded edge of the quilt and binding should match.

3 Stitch with the quilt on top, the binding on the bottom.

4 Start stitching at a corner. Leave long thread tails to hand knot at the end of the stitching.

5 The right stitch falls off the fabrics, while the left stitch catches the fold of the quilt. Adjust the zigzag width to securely catch the folds without stitching through the batting.

6 Stitch to the corner and stop with the needle out of the fabrics. Do not cut the threads.

7 Pull the quilt from under the presser foot, until the quilt is at least three inches from the foot. Fold the quilt to line up with the next side of the binding.

8 Loop the threads around your left fingers and slide the quilt and binding under the foot. Pull the thread tails taut. Start stitching at the corner. Continue around the quilt.

9 Hand knot the thread tails on all four corners. Using a large hand sewing needle pull the thread tails between the quilt and binding.

If the seam doesn't lie flat, loosen the top tension. Loosening the top tension allows wider stitch widths to lie flat.

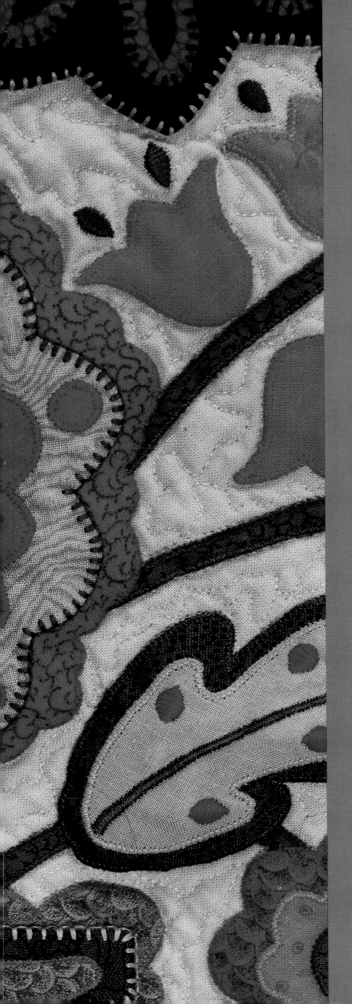

Part Five

APPLIQUÉ
PATTERNS

Floral Urns **quilt by Debra Wagner**

CHAPTER 16
Appliquéd Baskets and Christmas Wreath

WHEN YOU HAVE FINISHED practicing on samples,
you might want to try your new appliqué and binding skills using the
complex patterns presented here.

PATTERNS FROM *FLORAL URNS*

The three pattern blocks that follow are from my quilt *Floral Urns*. This quilt won the Bernina Award for Machine Workmanship at the Ninth Annual American Quilter's Society Quilt Show in 1993. The charming floral motifs of this pattern are inspired by the folk designs of Hungary, Poland, and Czechoslovakia. I used an assortment of small monotone prints for the appliqués and a warm cream color for the back-

ground. The finished size of the blocks is 15" square.

I'm not providing an exact duplicate of my quilt so that you can develop your own combinations for the rest of your blocks. This is a creative challenge to you to add your own flower and leaf shapes, as well as butterflies, other urn decorations, and whatever else suits your fancy.

USING *FLORAL URNS* PATTERNS

This collection of patterns uses the techniques from the appliqué

chapters in Part Two. The blocks are machine appliquéd and embellished. The designs are based on antique album quilt blocks and Berlin wool work. Each quarter of each block pattern is presented full-size to make a 15" block. Make a copy and assemble the pattern parts to make the full size patterns. You can further enlarge or reduce these patterns, but be aware that smaller sizes can be difficult to work.

SCALLOP BASKET
UPPER LEFT

SCALLOP BASKET
UPPER RIGHT

SCALLOP BASKET
LOWER LEFT

SCALLOP BASKET
LOWER RIGHT

JINGLE BELL BASKET
UPPER LEFT

JINGLE BELL BASKET
UPPER RIGHT

JINGLE BELL BASKET
LOWER LEFT

JINGLE BELL BASKET
LOWER RIGHT

BUBBLE GUM BASKET
UPPER LEFT

BUBBLE GUM BASKET
UPPER RIGHT

BUBBLE GUM BASKET
LOWER LEFT

BUBBLE GUM BASKET
LOWER RIGHT

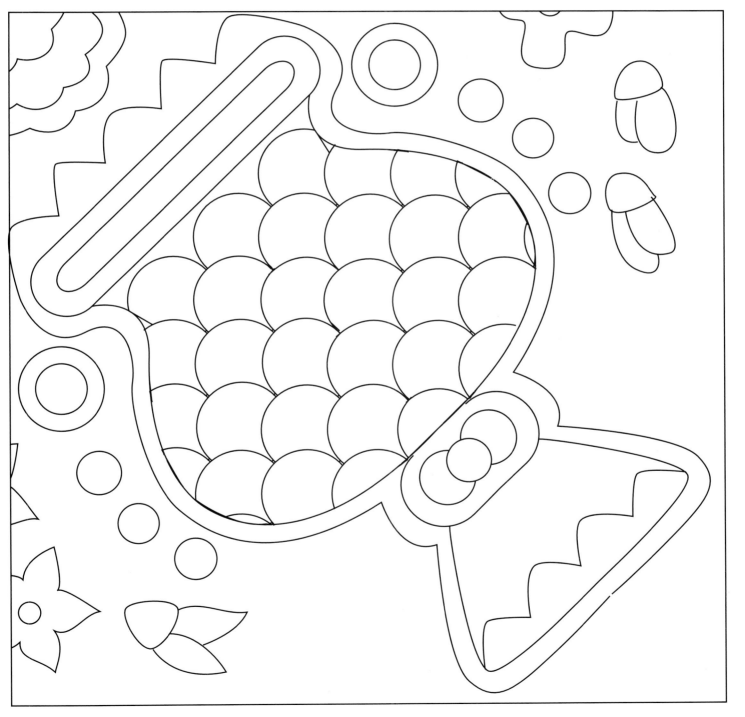

Christmas Wreath wallhanging by Deb Wagner.

BONUS CHRISTMAS WREATH PATTERN

The following pattern is from a winter wall hanging that is part of a set of season blocks I am making for commission. The owner graciously allowed me to share this breathtaking pattern with you. It is one of my favorite patterns. The shapes of the bow and poinsettias make this a classic winter design. The pattern was inspired by antique Berlin wool work and the needlepoint designs of Elizabeth Bradley. The reds, whites, and greens are stunning against a cream background. I used all solid colors.

When making a sample, I used raw edge appliqué and backed the light colors with lightweight fusible interfacing to keep the dark colors from shadowing through. The quarter-pattern pieces provided would result in a 15" block, which is too hard to work. I suggest that you enlarge it to at least a 22" square, or the pieces will be too small to handle. Enjoy!

Detail of *Christmas Wreath* wallhanging.

CHRISTMAS WREATH
UPPER LEFT

CHRISTMAS WREATH
UPPER RIGHT

CHRISTMAS WREATH
LOWER LEFT

CHRISTMAS WREATH
LOWER RIGHT

Bibliography

Bradley, Elizabeth. *Decorative Victorian Needlework*. New York, N.Y.: Clarkson N. Potter, Inc., 1990.

Sienkiewicz, Elly. *Baltimore Beauties and Beyond, Volume One*. Lafayette, Ca.: C&T Publishing, 1989.

———. *Baltimore Album Quilts*. Lafayette, Ca.: C&T Publishing, 1990.

———. *Baltimore Beauties and Beyond, Volume Two*. Lafayette, Ca.: C&T Publishing, 1991.

———. *Design A Baltimore Album Quilt!*. Lafayette, Ca.: C&T Publishing, 1992.

———. *Dimensional Appliqué*. Lafayette, Ca.: C&T Publishing, 1993.

Resource List

Clotilde Inc.
1909 S.W. First Avenue
Fort Lauderdale, FL 33315
Sewing notions and presser feet

Curiosity
19730 Top O' The Moor Drive
Monument, CO 80132
Appliqué patterns

Nancy's Notions
Dept. 25564, P.O. Box 63
Beaver Dam, WI 53916
Sewing notions and presser feet

Sewing Emporium
1087 Third Avenue
Chula Vista, CA 92010
Presser feet and other sewing supplies

Index